PORTUGAL: BIRTH OF A DEMOCRACY

PORTUGAL:
BIRTH OF A DEMOCRACY

Robert Harvey

St. Martin's Press · New York

Printed in Great Britain
Library of Congress Catalog Card Number 78-4507
ISBN 0-312-63184-7
First published in the United States of America in 1978

Library of Congress Cataloging in Publication Data

Harvey, Robert, 1953–
   Portugal—birth of a democracy
   Includes index

   1. Portugal—History—Revolution, 1974.
   2. Portugal—History—1974–
   I. Title
DP680.H38   946.9′044   78-4507
ISBN 0-312-63184-7

FOR JANE

Contents

List of abbreviations

CAP	Confederation of Portuguese Farmers
CDS	Centre Democratic Party
CIA	Central Intelligence Agency
CIP	Confederation of Portuguese Industry
COPCON	Operational Command for the Continent
DGS	Directorate-General of Security
EEC	European Economic Community
ELP	Portuguese Liberation Army
FLA	Front for the Liberation of the Azores
FMU	United Military Front
FNAT	National Federation for Joy at Work
FNLA	National Front for the Liberation of Angola
FRELIMO	Front for the Liberation of Mozambique
FUMO	United Democratic Front of Mozambique
IARN	Institute for Aid to National Refugees
IMF	International Monetary Fund
LUAR	League of United Revolutionary Action
MDLP	Democratic Movement for the Liberation of Portugal
MDP	Portuguese Democratic Movement
MFA	Armed Forces Movement
MPLA	Popular Movement for the Liberation of Angola
MRPP	Movement for the Reorganisation of the Portuguese Proletariat
NATO	North Atlantic Treaty Organisation
OECD	Organisation for Economic Co-operation and Development
PIDE	International Police for the Defence of the State
PPD (later PSD)	Popular Democratic Party (later Social Democratic Party)
PRP/BR	People's Revolutionary Party/Revolutionary Brigades
RALI-I	First Light Artillery Regiment
SUV	Soldiers United Will Win
UNITA	National Union for the Total Independence of Angola

1 Laboratory of Revolution

Portugal is a peanut of a country. Its total land area of 34,000 square miles is less than that of Scotland. Its population at the last census was just over 8 million people—less than the population of greater London. Its capital of Lisbon has only 800,000 people, less than the population of a medium-sized English city. Portugal's other major city, Oporto, has only 300,000 people. For fifty years of dictatorship it was a backward, neglected corner of Europe, its economic expansion, even the ferocity of its authoritarian ruler, overshadowed by those of its larger neighbour, Spain. Its economic and social structures were almost feudal. Most of Portugal's people lived in and around villages of less than 100 people, and only one-third lived in towns of over 5000 people.

Portugal's industrial expansion had been hamstrung by the tight monetarist policies of its dictator, Antonio Salazar, and by the stagnation of enterprise under the small monopolist group that dominated the country's banking and industry. Most of Portugal's industry, trade and farming in the north was small-scale—more than half of the labour force was employed in units of ten people or less. Most Portuguese firms were traditional and inefficient, competitive only because of the low cost of wages. Except in certain developed areas, near Lisbon and in the Algarve in the south, the country's tourist potential had hardly been touched. More than any other country in Western Europe, Portugal's was still a peasant economy. The middle class that grew up in Spain after the 1960s hardly materialised in Portugal. What middle class there was came largely from the professions and service industries connected with the government. Salazar treated Portugal like an only daughter, keeping her away from the outside world so that she would lead a maidenly existence and look after him in his old age.

But some maiden daughters go wild after the old man dies. The extrovert abandon of Portugal's revolutionary experience after April 1974, and the country's flirtations with all types of undesirables, shocked Europe and the world into suddenly sitting up and taking an interest in what was happening in Portugal. Portugal's novel experiments in government and society yielded enough material to absorb a generation of political and social historians.

In 1974, the country was taken over by a left-wing group of army captains, similar in some respects to the cliques that seized power in Egypt in 1952 and in Libya in 1969. The captains tested out orthodox

Soviet-style communism, and idealistic 'popular power' style assemblies. They tried government by committee, by officers' assembly, by triumvirate. They attempted to transform an army from an organisation based on discipline to one based on ideology—with disastrous results. They experimented with workers' control of industry, with mass expropriation of land, with nationalisation. Two coups, one failed coup, and a successful counter-coup, took place in rapid succession over the space of two years. A prime minister was driven from office by an overwhelming popular revolt against him, and his successor went on strike as prime minister when a major confrontation with the unions threatened to drive him from office. Every major political freedom—of expression, of the press, of the right to strike, of assembly, of the judiciary—was debated, discussed, wrangled over and eventually established in the course of the Portuguese revolution. What started as a coup became a revolution which was stopped by a reaction before it became an anarchy. Out of the tumult a democracy was born.

Portugal became a centre of attention in Europe and the world not just because of the freakish quality of its democratic experiment, but because the people won in the end. The attempt to replace a right-wing dictatorship with a left-wing one failed because the great mass of Portuguese rebelled against the idea of exchanging one master for another. The armed forces, which had propped up Salazar's dictatorship for so long, replaced his successor in 1974 as if they had been in no way responsible for the regime's durability. They called themselves liberators on 25 April 1974, but almost immediately assigned to themselves the task of deciding what was best for the people they had liberated. But the Portuguese rose up behind a group of tenacious civilian politicians and together they proved stronger than the political minority running the army, which eventually yielded power in surprise to a group of professional officers prepared to hand over power to the civilians.

How long the people's representatives will stay in control still remains to be seen. The soldiers, although smarting from their rebuff from the people, have not lost their interest in politics yet. But Portugal was proof at least that political rule cannot be wholly imposed from above. That silent minorities, when prodded too far, can become vocal. That democracy is still an ideal capable of stirring as much passion in the hearts of the masses as the economic self-interest usually cited by extremist ideologies as the motive force of political action. The Salazarist ethic had been that dictatorship survives if people are just sufficiently provided for to stay quiet, and if the social structure is kept unchanged. And the far-left ethic on the other hand was that democracy and freedom are bourgeois ideals in which the masses are uninterested, provided they get equal economic justice. Both were shown by the Portuguese people between 1974 and 1976 to have presumptuously false foundations.

It was a surprise to both extremes that democracy should assert itself so forcibly in a country without a large middle class. The Marxist view, that bourgeois dictatorship is the natural historical precursor of proletarian revolution, has rarely been confirmed. Most revolutions, in those few countries such as Russia, China and Cuba where they have not been imposed by force of foreign arms, have generally taken place in underdeveloped societies. Only in such societies has it been possible for a small minority to impose itself without facing the hostility of a large middle class. Portugal, then, might seem a revolutionary walk-over: through the early months of 1975 when political parties and conservative generals alike seemed unable to stop the drive of a deter-mined revolutionary minority towards the far left, the situation looked depressingly like that in Russia in 1917, when confusion on the right and in the centre allowed what was originally a tiny party, the Bolsheviks, to seize control of the main organs of power.

But the revolutionaries in Portugal ran up against the brick wall first of the Church's influence in northern Portugal and second of the system of landholdings there. The majority of northerners, who them-selves comprise 60 per cent of the people of Portugal, are smallholders and their families, clinging ferociously to tiny plots of land which offer them an adequate—if hardly consumer-oriented—standard of living. The smallholders felt themselves threatened by the onward march of land seizures by the far left in the south of the country, and the peasants rallied in the summer of 1975 to turn back the revolutionary tide. Most of the northern farmers were no better off than Portugal's urban labour force, but their land ownership gave them, in Marxist terminology, a bourgeois mentality. Underdeveloped as Portugal was, it had a very large class of people who would inevitably feel themselves threatened by a revolutionary seizure of power. Portugal's old right-wing dictators were shocked to find revolutionaries quietly subverting their most reliable and stalwart conservative prop, the army, in the early 1970s; but after 1974 the country's revolutionaries were transfixed to discover that the impoverished Portuguese people were anything but revolution-ary, and capable even of fighting against revolution.

Nor were the Portuguese fighting just out of economic self-interest. When Portugal's electorate first went to the polls in April 1975, 38 per cent of them supported the Socialist party and 26 per cent the Popular Democratic party, both of which were then, in different degrees, preaching socialism. In the general elections held in April 1976, and in the local elections the following December, they voted for the same parties in only slightly lesser numbers, although the Socialists had shown themselves unsympathetic to many of the economic interests of those who had risen up against the Communists. But in both elections, both parties were identified with the struggle for liberty, the fight against left-wing dictatorship. The Portuguese were loyal to their democratic champions at least as long as they feared that democracy could still be lost.

The Portuguese revolution gave important insights into how an army can be radicalised. Armies are usually apolitical. Soldiery was an honourable profession in Portugal, but it never attracted the best political brains, because Portugal's soldiers, unlike many of Latin America's, had been perfectly content to let civilians run the country for most of the century. So a small minority of soldiers within the Portuguese army could, because of their command of key tactical positions, set the pace for the great mass of disunited soldiers. Training, background and military discipline usually mean that these political minorities have right-wing views. But Portugal was fighting a colonial war which was unpopular with the soldiers, particularly the professional ones. Their enemy had an ideology that was scarcely more profound than the Portuguese colonial logic, but which had more inherent appeal. The captains swallowed whole the simplistic theories of their African nationalist opponents, and proceeded to take advantage of the generalised dissatisfaction within the army to stage a military coup. The captains were only stopped in their revolutionary tracks when a popular revolt in the north and the advanced disintegration of the Portuguese army created a reaction among previously impartial professional soldiers.

Portugal's revolution had a dramatic international impact. It was, of course, colonial war that stirred Portugal's captains to rise up in 1975, and nothing in Portugal's revolution will be more lasting than the manner of its decolonisation. Cathartic and abrupt, Portuguese decolonisation left Angola a prey to civil war, and Mozambique in the hands of a Marxist ruler whose collectivist policies have not been rivalled elsewhere in Africa. In Angola, the Portuguese high commission actively smoothed the way for a Marxist victory. And when confrontation eventually broke out between the three Angolan nationalist movements staking their claims to the country for which they had jointly fought Portugal for so long, the first major intervention of a large foreign army in Africa since colonial days—15,000 Cubans— took place. The civil war threatened to foreshadow the long-feared South African racial war. The takeover of Angola and Mozambique finally destroyed Rhodesia's chances of being able to withstand a prolonged struggle against total encirclement by well-trained, well-equipped and well-financed guerrillas. And for the first time it called into question the very survival of white South Africa.

The shattering effect of Portugal's coup on South Africa's troubled peace is outside the scope of this book. But decolonisation had profoundly negative effects within Portugal itself. Disagreement as to the best way of pulling out of the colonies was a major element in the early power struggle between right and left in Portugal. Decolonisation increased Portugal's population by more than one-tenth—as settlers who had gone to build new lives in Africa fled the repression of their new rulers, leaving all their possessions behind. Decolonisation left the Portuguese, always an ambitious people, without a role. Until 1974 they had been, as Salazar never ceased to remind them, the proud possessors of an empire larger than all of Western Europe; now they were just a backward appendage to the continent from which they had so long averted their gaze.

The answer was to seek out and join Western Europe. From outside, the Portuguese looked at the promised land and put their faith in everything that the European Common Market is not—a political organisation with a coherent sense of identity. They had to believe in Europe because there was nothing else to believe in. All three of Portugal's democratic political parties pledged themselves to the European ideal, although Europe then had little to offer them economically and little to offer anyone politically. The faith that little Portugal invested in the shambling colossus of the Community did, however, almost shame it into doing something. European political parties did actually shell out money and support for Portugal's democratic parties. At international conferences European leaders dressed down the soldiers who were preparing to take away Portugal's barely glimpsed freedom. Even loans to a struggling Portugal—not much, but a start is a start—were forthcoming.

Grudgingly, and perhaps for the first time, European leaders took the wholly political decision of overcoming their economic misgivings and giving a cautious welcome to Portugal's entry into the Common Market, although it remains to be seen whether this will eventually be blocked. Not because of anything the Community had done, but because of what it stood for, because another country had idealised it, a very real contribution had been made to the victory of the democratic forces in that country. How long the Portuguese suitor will be deceived by the surface beauty of the European idea, or whether she will reform her slovenly ways to match the high qualities expected of her by Portugal, will only become clear later.

Europe's interest was not, of course completely altruistic. Portugal's geographical position gave the country an important defence role in NATO. The American base at Lajes, in the Azores, monitors Russian submarine movements in the Atlantic, and is crucial to the defence of the area. Portugal's incomparable deep-water ports could be a powerful help to NATO in the event of a war. Portugal had played a major part in the 1973 Middle Eastern war by allowing American planes carrying supplies to Israel to refuel in the Portuguese-owned Azores islands when other oil-conscious Western European countries refused.

Above all, though, the threat that a left-wing military dictatorship backed by the Communist party would come to power in Portugal would have seriously undermined the credibility of the NATO alliance. Portugal would have been the first NATO member that the alliance could no longer trust. The Americans might have considered open intervention to show the Russians that they could not tolerate any crumbling away at the fringes of the alliance, which might spread elsewhere, for example to Italy and France. But direct American intervention would have had disastrous effects for America's image at home and abroad, which is why the Americans would probably have shrunk from such action. If they had quietly given up, the Russians might have drawn the lesson that the Americans were not prepared to resort to Russian methods to ensure total obedience among other European allies. And the Russians might have tried to pick another European plum.

The next plum that might have been attempted, although almost certainly with results equally disastrous both to Russia and to democracy, was Spain. Spain's tough, unpoliticised professional army would have almost certainly withstood any Communist attempts to infiltrate it, or to bring about a revolution. But if the Communists had stirred things up there, they would have had little trouble in provoking a repressive right-wing military coup. As it was, the failure of Portugal's Communists to take power by revolutionary means reinforced those Communists who argued in Italy, France and Spain that Communism must come to power by behaving democratically.

And Portugal's experience taught Spain's leaders a lot of other lessons. Spain's new king was given a vivid display next door of what happens when a dictatorship liberalises too slowly: it gets the conservatives' backs up, while frustrating the democrats and allowing the extremes to organise themselves. You can repress all of the people all of the time; you can free all of the people all of the time; but you can't repress some of the people some of the time. Marcello Caetano, Portugal's last right-wing dictator, was a cautious reformist who tried to let the steam out gradually from Salazar's dangerously overheating military dictatorship. But he stood too close and was scalded.

Spain's rulers were right, after only a moment's hesitation, to take the valve off completely, and then jump well clear. The government earned itself popularity and took Spain's extremes by surprise. The far left suddenly had no prison bars left to rattle; while the army could not complain that Spain was being taken over by the far left. Which leads to the second lesson for Spain of the Portuguese revolution: that democracy, far from being the forerunner of revolution, may be the best safeguard against it. It was the people, who by their 71 per cent vote for the democratic parties in April 1975, and their uprising in the north during the following summer, stopped Portugal from being taken over by a clique of left-wing extremists in army uniform. It was the people in whom King Juan Carlos of Spain and his prime minister, Adolfo Suarez, put their trust when they took the calculated gamble of dismantling an army dictatorship. And by their mass vote for the centre parties in Spain's general election of June 1977, the people did not disappoint the moderates' expectations.

The Portuguese experience taught a few international lessons as well. It taught the Americans restraint. Because of the accident that Portugal's revolution took place at the time when the covert actions of the Central Intelligence Agency were being exposed to the glare of Senate hearing and television spotlights, the Americans were inhibited from making the kind of overkill to counter far-left revolutionaries that they had previously made elsewhere. It is open to doubt whether covert American operations in different parts of the world have furthered American interests. In Chile, for example, between 1970 and 1973, the reaction within the armed forces against the Marxist regime of Salvador Allende made a coup there all but inevitable, and made the $8 million which the CIA spent there on 'destabilising' operations largely superfluous. The Americans were quite unnecessarily tainted with the brush of interfering in another country's internal affairs, when a policy of non-intervention would have probably yielded much the same results. Since the coup in Chile, indeed, the Americans have been wholly unable to control the excesses of the military dictatorship they were supposed to have brought to power.

In Portugal, the Americans adopted a low profile, and it paid off. Given enough rope, the revolutionaries hanged themselves. By their excesses they alienated the large bulk of the Portuguese people, and all the country's democratic parties, including Mario Soares's mainstream Socialist party. When the reckoning eventually came, it was at the hands of a dour professional soldier allied to the Socialists, who believed that the army should get out of politics. The Communists and the soldier radicals were thrown out by the people first, and by the democratic parties second, and only lastly by the right-wing soldiers. No one could argue that the brutal military friends of the Americans had suppressed democracy in Portugal. There was, of course, American aid for Portugal's democrats, to counter the extensive Russian aid flowing, with meagre electoral results to show for it, to the Communist party. But American help was discreet, and above all it went to help the democratic forces in Portugal, not to anti-democratic groups in the army or extreme right-wingers, as in Chile. You don't make enemies if you don't openly mess around in other countries' affairs until there is absolutely no alternative, was the message Portugal sent to America.

The Portuguese experience also had a limited impact on what will probably be Europe's biggest headache over the coming decade—the problem of southern European Communists. Since the success of Europe's pioneer democratic Communist party, Italy's, in local elections in June 1975, one Western European Communist party after another has been rallying round to express its belief in pluralist democracy. The notable exception has been Portugal's, which bluntly sticks to the belief that Western democracy is bourgeois and therefore no democracy at all, and that real democracy will only be achieved when the dictatorship of the proletariat destroys class divisions altogether. Alvaro Cunhal, the Portuguese Communist party secretary, is still unrepentantly pro-Stalinist and will not suffer a word said in anger about the treatment of political dissidents in Russia. True to his principles, Cunhal, alone of all main Portuguese party leaders, hitched the Communists to the bandwagon of the far-leftists and Communists who attempted to install a military dictatorship in Portugal in 1975.

The Portuguese line was intensely embarrassing to the Italian Communists, who were trying to persuade Italian voters that Western European Communists were something different from Eastern European Communists, and to the French Communists, who had an electoral pact with the Socialist party. The unity of the French left-wing alliance was stretched to the limits, as the Communist leader Georges Marchais, declared his faith in Cunhal's revolutionary line while François Mitterand, the Socialist leader, echoed the warnings of Portugal's Socialist leader, Mario Soares, against a dictatorship propped up by the Communists in Portugal. None of these divisions have proved lasting. But the Portuguese Communists' obstinate refusal to join the rest of the herd is a perpetual reminder to Western Communists that Communism and democracy do not necessarily go together.

The outcome of Portugal's democratic experiment will continue to be important to Western Europe, and especially the Hispanic world. If it fails, and a military dictatorship moves in once again, it will lend credence to the almost racist, but among many Portuguese and Spaniards widely held, idea that Iberians are inherently incapable of democracy. A military coup in Portugal could have profound repercussions in Spain, where many officers still doubt the chances of democracy surviving long.

Even so, too close a comparison should not be drawn between the democratic experiments in Portugal and Spain. Spain's democratic experiment is following in the wake of an economic and social revolution that took place in the 1960s and has rendered its old political structure increasingly obsolete; in a sense the political development of Spain is merely catching up with the changes in Spanish society that have brought it up to date with the rest of Western Europe. The dictatorship in Spain could not have gone on after Franco without a lot of blood being shed. In Portugal the old regime would probably have survived uninterrupted but for the colonial war; the political change has preceded the social one.

It was only because power in Portugal was concentrated in so few hands, because the country had no substantial middle class, that it was possible for the country to move so easily from one extreme to the other. The pendulum has come to settle in the centre, but could easily be dislodged again. Portugal's new democratic rulers have a much more difficult task than Spain's: that of transforming their society and economy into modern European ones, capable of gaining the popular support that democracy needs in order to survive. It can be done, if Portugal's small but talented class of politicians set the consolidation of democracy above party advantage, and if they are given enough time by the army.

2 The angry young captains

The crowds that turned out in Lisbon to greet Portugal's soldier liberators on 25 April 1974 thought they were applauding a revolution. But
they were only witnessing the changing of the guard. One faction in the
Portuguese army overthrew another faction, that was all. Ever since a
military coup on 17 June 1926 had put an end to sixteen years of
unstable parliamentary government, power in Portugal had always
lain with the army. Real power continued to lie with the soldiers even
after they put an austere conservative academic, Antonio Salazar, in
the post of finance minister in 1928 to handle an economic crisis that
was too much for them.

Salazar's success in restoring economic stability to the country, as
well as in forging a political and administrative basis for civilian government, became his enduring credential to govern. He was appointed
prime minister in 1932. Meanwhile military power was institutionalised
in the office of the president, which General Carmona, who led the 1926
coup, held until his death in 1951. The president could dismiss the
prime minister at will under Article 82 of the 1933 constitution, promul-
gated under Salazar. The army had the real power, but it preferred to
leave the business of government and administration to civilians, as
long as two broad conditions were fulfilled: first, that the government
did not interfere with the military's own special status and interests,
and second that the government continued to maintain economic and
public order.

Portugal's soldiers had little cause for complaint under Dr Salazar.
After a period of raging inflation under the old Republic, caused
largely through printing money on a vast scale to finance impractical
and often corruptly administered government projects, Salazar embarked on a policy of stringent monetary control. For the first time in
fifteen years, in the financial year 1928/29, he balanced the government
budget. An annual deficit of about $6 million was turned into a surplus
of $30,000. The Portuguese economy was put into a straitjacket, which
made it easier to control, but much more difficult to develop. At
the time, though, Salazar's achievement looked like something of a
miracle, and the officers congratulated themselves for having chosen so
well.

Chosen, too, in a way which protected the conservative interests of
the senior officers, many of whom came from landowning families, or

belonged to one of the small oligarchic dynasty that monopolised most of Portuguese banking and industry. The Control of Industry Act (Lei de Condicionamento Industrial) provided the mechanism for preserving control in the hands of a select group—like the Champalimaud and Cuf empires: monopolies in certain fields were actively conceded by the government, and new development by smaller groups was rigorously controlled. The difficulty of obtaining credit at reasonable rates of interest—a consequence of Salazarian austerity—made it extremely difficult for small entrepreneurs to break into the market dominated by the traditional giants. Salazar pickled the existing economic and social order in a monetary jar. He compared himself to 'a good housekeeper, knowing how to spend well what one has, and not spend more than one's resources can afford'.

The prime minister did nothing to create his own political power base and lessen his dependence on the army. The popular institutions he set up were the least necessary for the peaceful working of government. The political party he created, the Uniao Nacional (National Union), subscribed to a few corporativist ideals that had blown over from Mussolini's Italy—but never attempted to put them into practice. The politicians were anyway ignored, as so often in Portugal, by the country's real rulers—Salazar and the army behind him. Elections to the national assembly set up under the 1933 constitution were guaranteed to deliver a majority to National Union candidates. The official results registered considerable support for the opposition, making them appear more credible than rigged elections under other dictatorships. The only significant opposition campaign was mounted by General Humberto Delgado, who ran for president in 1958, but was defeated on a fixed vote and later murdered by Salazar's secret police.

Indeed Salazar's only independent support came from the security service created in 1927 to fight political subversion. With an estimated 3000 full-time agents and a much wider net of political informers, the PIDE, which was renamed the Directorate-General of Security—DGS —after Salazar's death, proved adequate to the task of driving left-wing forces underground. It proved rather less effective, as events were to show, in counteracting subversive trends in the armed forces.

In the 1960s, pressures began to emerge for a change in Salazar's economic system. The Portuguese economy began to develop away from its old Salazarist dualism, based on agricultural production and the importation and re-export of raw materials from the colonies. This was partly due to a slump in markets for primary products, and partly due to the growth in world trade after the war. Portuguese investors began to diversify into heavy industry within Portugal itself, based on a cheap, non-unionised labour force. Foreign capital investment began to grow, particularly in such fields as transport, electrical machinery, mineral and paper production. It would be an over-simplification to say that there was a direct clash between the new industrial interests and the old colonial-agricultural economic lobby, because many of the new fortunes were made by channelling the old capital into the new industries. But the Portuguese economy began to depend less on its colonial and agricultural trade, and correspondingly fewer businessmen considered that the heavy cost of maintaining Portugal's colonies was worth the diminishing economic returns.

This transformation of the nature of Portuguese capitalism did not cause the military coup of April 1974: a group of soldiers from lower-middle-class backgrounds with immediate service grievances did that. But the transformation created a climate in which empire was no longer the *sine qua non* of wealth in Portugal. And so one of Salazar's oldest props, his capitalist upper middle class, had all but stopped supporting the Portuguese commitment to empire under his successor, Marcello Caetano. This evolution of Portuguese capitalism helps to explain the singular lack of capitalist reaction against the April coup. The small size of Portugal's monopolist capitalist middle class also helps to explain why Portugal was able to go off on such a revolutionary tangent after April 1974 without arousing a more immediate and violent reaction than the one it eventually did.

The equation that allowed a contented army to prop up a civilian dictatorship also began to change in the 1960s. Salazar was an inflexible colonialist and had little time for the independence movements that grew up in the major colonies of Portuguese Africa—Mozambique, Angola, Guinea and Guinea-Bissau. Salazar considered the colonies part of Portugal itself—'the whole territory of Portugal'—and refused to consider even a gradualist approach towards independence. The colonies, after all, gave Portugal its chief claim to world importance; and counter-insurgency operations by Portuguese troops in the early 1960s suggested that the colonial situation should be kept under control everywhere except in Guinea-Bissau. But the financial cost of the operation began to tell, and to pare down Salazar's reputation as an economic miracle-worker. The mounting cost in human lives, coupled with Portugal's abnormally long period of compulsory military service —four years—began to weary the Portuguese people.

Not least, new questions were raised in the minds of the professional soldiers in the field. Young officers, isolated from contact with European armies and European ideas, became increasingly aware of the idealistic Marxism of the liberation movements they were fighting. Faced by an apparently endless and unwinnable war under difficult conditions, the officers began to wonder what they were doing there at all. Their grievances were fuelled by a new military decree thoughtlessly passed by Salazar's successor, Dr Marcello Caetano, in July 1973, improving promotion prospects for conscript officers. In trying to appease growing popular resentment against military service in Africa, Caetano had provoked a much more dangerous enemy: the professional officer class which had had to work long and hard for its own promotions. There was a class grievance too: the professional officers usually came from families too poor to gain their education except through the army. The conscript officers were generally reasonably well-educated university graduates.

Although no one realised it at the time, the professional officers were the natural malcontents of the Salazar regime. Economic stringency—or stagnation—prevented the emergence of anything like the substantial middle class that was growing up in Spain at the beginning of the 1960s. The class that usually acts as a breeding ground for political opposition was extremely small in Portugal. The armed forces instead became the obvious channel for ambition, because promotion and status could be achieved on the basis of merit. The potential for what Marxists call bourgeois revolution did not exist in Portuguese society itself—the bourgeoisie was too small—but in the armed forces, a large part of which served abroad. The division between the senior conservative officers who backed the old regime, and the junior officers, in many cases from petty bourgeois backgrounds, was a very wide one.

Out of a class division, fomented by immediate grievances, came an army revolution. The initial architects of the revolution showed no particular concern for democratic rights in Portugal. They were not interested in replacing military control with popular control, or dictatorship with democracy. They were concerned, first, to overthrow the conservative generals running the armed forces, and, secondly, to destroy the existing social and economic structure in Portugal, which had invidiously concentrated wealth and power in a select few hands; they wanted a new power structure to reflect their own interests. And most of these revolutionary middle-ranking officers espoused the Marxism of their African opponents as the obvious opposite of everything they disliked about the government in power in Portugal.

They were wrong, on their own terms. Marx had argued that a proletarian revolution was only possible after a bourgeois revolution had overthrown a country's feudal power structure, and had set in motion the system of capital concentration which would politicise the masses forced to work under it. Only when the proletariat was urbanised and exploited would a strong enough political consciousness and a political solidarity materialise which could eventually overthrow the capitalist state. But Portugal, in crude Marxist terms, was still in the feudal phase. By April 1974, most of Portugal's people lived outside the big towns. Some 47 per cent of people were engaged in agriculture, compared to

26·7 per cent in service industries, and 25 per cent in industry. Portugal's economy was suffering from the concentration of power in a few hands, not from the ruthless market exploitation of private enterprise. Even on a Marxist analysis of Portugal's economic and social development, the soldiers were making a mistake in trying to enforce Marxist solutions. But, then, Marxism was just the fashionable political creed they latched on to when their own grievances forced them into opposition to the political and economic clique then ruling Portugal.

The Movimento das Forcas Armadas—the Armed Forces Movement (MFA)—was born out of army discontent, political ignorance, and barely understood Marxist ideology. Very few of the dissident officers had read much around the ideology they were championing, and still fewer were committed Communists. The exceptions were led by Colonel Vasco Goncalves, an officer in the army engineering corps. Goncalves had a long record of political activity. In 1958 he joined General Humberto Delgado's Independent Military Movement, a clandestine anti-Salazarist organisation. Even then, his brother officers were convinced he was a card-carrying member of the Communist party. He was a capable, intelligent officer with a distinguished record on his tours of duty overseas. But he was too hard, lean and dour to be generally popular among his colleagues, and he had a lashing, sarcastic tongue they disliked. He was prone to moods of deep depression and at other times could become heated and over-excited, qualities that were to become apparent when he became a public figure. He was the most senior officer to join the MFA.

Another highly political officer to join the Movement, in late 1973, was Major Melo Antunes. The major was much more vocal about his left-wing opinions than the taciturn Goncalves, and at first looked on the MFA as 'a reactionary co-operative of privilege'. He was unemotional, calculating, highly intelligent and widely read, and had studied Marxism when doing a course on subversive warfare at Lisbon's institute for higher military studies. He was a convinced Marxist, but he did not share Goncalves's enthusiasm for Soviet-style Communism. Instead, he preferred to evolve his own version of a 'third world' Socialism to which he felt backward Portugal and its colonies could subscribe.

One of the founders of the MFA was Major Vitor Alves, who had served in both Angola and Mozambique and was deeply interested in the social problems of these countries and in Portugal's justification for staying in the colonies. Also widely read, he was a gentle, reflective, humorous man, who seemed a little out of place in the army. He was less the committed Marxist than Antunes, but his social views were close enough to the latter's to forge an almost indissoluble bond over the next two years.

The leading planner, as well as the best publicist within the MFA, was Captain Otelo Saraiva de Carvalho. Otelo, as he was almost universally known, was a warm, amusing personality, who combined a ready smile with a good deal of strong-arm bluster. He confessed that he would have liked to have been an actor. His bonhomie made him a natural leader of men—but in an unusual direction. Otelo's political views, he said, were formed when 'My men complained of fighting abroad, of the pittance they were paid. I said: "Why do you do it, then?" And I knew I had to fight for them.' Otelo's political theories, such as they were, came from reading the revolutionary guerrilla manuals of his enemies in the African bush, and he was a firm admirer of Fidel Castro and Che Guevara. Fortunately, he lacked the ruthlessness of either man.

The MFA first came together as an entity on 9 September 1973, when 15 army officers arranged a meeting for some 121 others at a farmhouse about twenty miles from the town of Evora in south-eastern Portugal, to discuss their grievances and opposition to the war. The officers confined themselves to sending a resolution to the army chief of staff, General Costa Gomes, who was known to sympathise with their professional grievances. But nothing came of Costa Gomes's representations to the prime minister, Caetano. So a second meeting was held on 6 October, where a co-ordinating committee was formed to run the Movement, and branches of the air force and navy were represented. Meetings took place with increasing frequency over the ensuing months and in December the 200 or so participants began to discuss the possibility of staging a military coup, but in the end voted to confine their protests to legal ones. The left-wingers in the movement, after the vote, managed to introduce an amendment, which allowed only those attending MFA meetings to vote, and not to act as proxies for non-attending officers. By this means the MFA became a less representative group of officers, but one much more efficient than the sprawling organisation of before. Spearheaded by Otelo, Goncalves and Antunes, the MFA co-ordinating committee began to plan for a coup.

The captains bided their time until February. The political activists were still a tiny fraction of the serving officer corps in the Portuguese armed forces, and a successful revolt was unthinkable without at least the tacit acquiescence of the majority. The majority were non-political professional soldiers, without any ideology, without any commitment to the existing regime beyond those of military discipline and subservience to the authorities in power. They shared the grievances of the Marxist officers, but not their creed, and had anyway been imbued after fifty years of Salazar with a vague but lasting distrust of Marxism. 'You could lead many of them anywhere, as long as it took them away from the old dictatorship, and stopped short of Communism,' one of the

MFA's early leaders, Major Vitor Alves, told the author. To succeed, a popular military figurehead was needed with a professional appeal for the non-political officers. He would need to be a senior officer, to lend legitimacy to a movement which would otherwise upset the established rules of military hierarchy if commanded by junior officers.

An internal power struggle among Portugal's leading generals was to provide the junior officers with their figurehead. Since 1958 Admiral Americo Thomaz had been the ceremonial but politically inactive president of Portugal. Although Thomaz embodied the power of the armed forces, Salazar's years in office had invested the old dictator with an authority which the armed forces were unwilling to contest. When Salazar retired through ill-health in 1968, and Professor Marcello Caetano came to office, the magic had gone. Leading officers wanted to play a significant role in ruling Portugal, and naturally aspired to the office of president. As the shadows lengthened on the old regime, the increasingly debilitated President Thomaz found himself presiding over a duel for the succession. On the right, General Kaulza de Arriaga, the Commander of Portuguese forces in Mozambique, returned to Lisbon in 1973 and privately published a book, *The Portuguese Answer*, which defended the Portuguese colonial presence in crudely simplistic terms:

> There are three basic causes of the strategic-political upheavals which we see occurring in so many different parts of the world. First there is the racism, or to be more exact, the neo-racism of the non-white man against the white man. Second there is banditry organised at international level. Third there is aggressive Communist imperialism, or more precisely, Communist neo-imperialism.

According to Kaulza, Communism was manipulating the first two forces to take over first Africa, and then Latin America; and so to isolate the United States and Europe as an enclave of whites in a segregated world. The Portuguese 'answer' was to try to build genuinely multi-racial societies in Africa to prevent this new form of world 'Apartheid' emerging, and to maintain the links between Europe and Africa. General Kaulza ends his book with the quixotic assertion: 'In Mozambique itself the present war cannot now be lost. It is only a question of time before it is fully won.' He was clearly pitching for the office of a president whose time had almost come.

Kaulza may have had some promises of support among senior officers. But his arguments had nothing like the impact of those of his chief rival for the job, General Antonio de Spinola. Spinola was a man who treated soldiery like politics: his style of leadership was based on personality, personal visits to isolated units in the jungle, personal morale-boosting, an engaging interest in the daily lives and social problems of his men. And his personality was based on show: he was a vain man, who enjoyed being the centre of attention, and would go to considerable lengths to make himself recognised, carefully cultivating personal trademarks—such as a rakishly tilted beret and Prussian-style monocle, which were as alien to the Portuguese officer corps as to any other Western European officer corps.

The general came from a distinguished civil service family, served in the cavalry, and after serving as military governor of Lisbon and as cavalry commander in Angola, became in May 1968 the governor and commander-in-chief of Portuguese Guinea. By 1972 he returned to Lisbon with a reputation as a military hero, and began immediately to plan for higher things than the post of deputy chief of staff to which he had been assigned. He had a powerful ally in the prime minister, Marcello Caetano. Back in December 1972, the PIDE had unearthed a plot by right-wing generals to depose Caetano for his cautious programme of reforms in the colonies—which gave some sort of franchise to educated Africans, and gave Angola and Mozambique a more autonomous status. Caetano undoubtedly felt his own position threatened: Spinola could provide a rallying point within the armed forces for the prime minister's views.

On 22 February 1974, Spinola published his book *Portugal and the Future*, which reflected Caetano's ideas about the evolution of the Portuguese empire into a 'Lusitanian community built upon the progressive autonomy of all its parts', based on the principle of self-determination. Caetano and Spinola, in other words, wanted to introduce democracy into Portugal's colonial possessions, which they were confident would lead to their continued association with Portugal. The alternative—and here Spinola came into direct conflict with Kaulza's views—was to view the empire as a bastion of Western interests, which must be defended, and this was both impractical and mistaken. Spinola's book was an immediate bestseller, and its publication had clearly been vetted both by Caetano and Spinola's immediate superior, the chief of staff, General Costa Gomes.

Events moved rapidly after that. Kaulza de Arriaga and his friends immediately protested to the prime minister in the strongest terms possible. To appease them, Caetano, who had been informed of the existence, though not the scale, of the dissident movement within the armed forces, decided to disperse some of its ringleaders. On 8 March Melo Antunes and other perennial left-wing troublemakers were posted abroad. But the prime minister failed to satisfy the army hard-liners' thirst for culprits. Uniting around President Thomaz, they demanded that the prime minister go to the source of the attack upon the government's colonial policy, and fire Spinola. Otherwise, they hinted, Caetano might himself be replaced by the president. So, after Spinola and Costa Gomes had refused to show up at a meeting to endorse Caetano's colonial policy, they were dismissed on 14 March.

That same day had been provisionally marked out by Otelo as the day for a potential coup. But in the storm surrounding Spinola's departure, the plotters thought it wise to postpone their plans indefinitely. Unrest, though, was rife, and the MFA's writ did not run through the whole army. An officer from a unit at Lamego in northern Portugal contacted MFA leaders on the night of 8 March to say that his men were about to march on Lisbon, and Otelo decided to throw caution to the winds. He and three other officers drove off to raise units loyal to the MFA for an uprising that night, but when Otelo reached his destination, he found the officers unprepared and disorganised. One of Otelo's fellow conspirators, however, discovered the cavalry unit at Caldas da Rainha in a ready state to march, and 200 soldiers set off in ten armoured vehicles for Lisbon. Ten miles north of Lisbon, this solitary column of rebels was met on the road by units from the paramilitary Republican National Guard and the Seventh Cavalry, and—presage of coups to come!—surrendered without bloodshed. About 200 soldiers were arrested, although Otelo and other ringleaders were not even interrogated. The feeble nature of the attempt lulled the PIDE/DGS into believing that discontent was much less widespread than it was. Otelo knew the next attempt would have to be better organised, and would need a figurehead capable of carrying the great mass of loyal, non-political army officers. The ideal person for the task was, of course, General Spinola.

MFA leaders had been in touch with both Costa Gomes and Spinola as early as December 1973. At that time, an MFA officer, Vasco Lourenco, had performed a service for the chief of staff and his deputy by warning them that the MFA had been approached for support by Kaulza de Arriaga. The ultra-right had wanted to overthrow Caetano, Spinola and Costa Gomes in one fell swoop. In the event, nothing came of Kaulza's plotting, which never went beyond the verbal stage, but contact was maintained with Spinola by two leading members of the Co-ordinating Committee of the MFA, Vasco Lourenco and Otelo de Carvalho. After the publication of Spinola's book, and the failure of the attempted coup in March, the co-ordinating committee came to an unanimous decision: Spinola would be asked to lead them after the coup.

Spinola agreed to support the plotters in principle. But he insisted on keeping out of any operational planning, and baulked at the first MFA programme drawn up by Melo Antunes, which he described as being 'primitively Communist'. A second draft programme was written, which expunged most of the revolutionary rhetoric in the first document, and which pledged the MFA to holding free elections for a constituent assembly within a year, and to allowing free trades unions and a free press. Spinola was worried about a clause providing for the 'speedy adoption of measures which lead towards the administrative and political autonomy for the overseas territories' because he envisaged a slow process of decolonisation. So the clause was removed in the final version.

25 April was selected as the day of the coup by Otelo after soundings carried out by MFA officers revealed that a wide cross-section of the army, following the dismissal of Spinola, would not now resist a coup. Otelo himself was in charge of the operational planning of the coup, which was both practical and imaginative. The scheme was based on the fact that Lisbon, bordered on the south and east by the Tagus estuary, can be approached only along three major channels of communication—the Salazar bridge across the Tagus, the coast road to the seaside resorts of Cascais and Estoril in the west, and the roads running into Lisbon from the north. Otelo also bargained on the fact that the security forces were equipped for crowd control, but not military resistance, and were comparatively small. He proposed to occupy the strategic approaches to Lisbon, and take over key posts in the city such as broadcasting stations, the telephone exchange and ministries. No troops would, however, be sent to seize army barracks; most soldiers, he hoped, would come to his aid, or at least stay passive.

The signal for the coup was given at 12.25 a.m. on the night of 24 April, when Jose Vasconcelos, a popular announcer on Portugal's commercial radio station, Radio Clube Portuguesa, played the song 'Grandola Vila Morena'. Under orders from the coup's communication centre, the Santarem cavalry school north of Lisbon, Otelo's troops moved into action. Units stationed around Lisbon, in garrisons in central Portugal, and in Santarem itself occupied the centre of the city, including the ministries of defence, the interior and the navy, the civil and military airports, the broadcasting, telephone and electricity stations, and the central post office. Four people were killed later in the day in a panic burst of fire into a crowd by PIDE members sheltering in their headquarters in the Rua Mario Cardoso. Otherwise there were no serious casualties.

The day's most human drama came with the passing of power from the prime minister to the new *de facto* head of the army. Caetano, who had taken refuge inside the headquarters of his loyal Republican National Guard, the Carmo barracks, was asked to surrender by a young cavalry captain, Salguiero Maia. Caetano replied with dignity that he would yield only to Spinola himself. But when MFA officers reached Spinola's house bearing Caetano's surrender, the insurrection's armchair leader replied that he needed a full expression of confidence by army leaders before accepting command. As the senior serving officer on the co-ordinating committee, it fell to Colonel Vasco Goncalves to convey the MFA's accolade. At 5.45 p.m. that afternoon, Spinola drove to Carmo to accept Caetano's formal surrender, and the cheers of the 10,000-strong crowd outside. The following day, Caetano and ex-president Thomaz were flown to temporary exile in Madeira, from which they were later to leave for Brazil.

3 Summer's president, autumn's victim

General Spinola, though, had not made the revolution. The MFA radicals had. The realities of the new power line-up made themselves felt almost immediately after the coup. A formal power structure was set up at once, but was effectively bypassed before it had begun to function. At the head of the pyramid was the interim president, General Spinola. Below him, there was a six-man Junta of National Salvation, consisting of Spinola, Brigadier Diogo Neto and General Galvao de Melo for the air force, Captains Pinheiro de Azevedo and Rosa Coutinho for the navy, and General Costa Gomes and Brigadier Silverio Marques for the army. Below that was the Council of State, which contained the entire Junta, the seven-man MFA co-ordinating committee and five 'outstanding Portuguese citizens', as well as two Spinolist aides, Colonel Almeida Bruno and Colonel Rafael Durao. This body, intended as an advisory constitutional body, was only inter-mittently consulted until its abolition in March 1975.

Below the Council of State came the provisional government, a coalition headed by Professor Palma Carlos, the conservative former dean of the law faculty at Lisbon university. The government contained ministers from the most organised political party to emerge immediately after the coup, the Communists; the disorganised but broadly based Socialist party; the Popular Democrats, which was the successor party to the former Liberal opposition under Caetano; and assorted inde-pendents.

In theory, the government was supposed to make the major executive and legislative decisions during the transitional phase before the elections the following spring, for an assembly which would draft a democratic constitution to be implemented the following autumn. In practice, cabinet disagreements between irreconcilable opposites para-lysed the government almost from the start: it became instead a symbolic and detached whispering gallery for the struggle taking place off the stage. The struggle, in its first stage, was to develop between General Spinola, almost alone, on the one hand, and the co-ordinating committee of the MFA on the other.

The contest was unequal from the start. Less than three months after the coup, an increasingly anxious Spinola made a bid to gain the initiative over the MFA radicals. Total disagreement within the cabinet between the centrists on the one hand, and the Communists and Socialists on the other, was emerging over the speed of decolonisation and the state of the Portuguese economy. Spinola, without success, attempted to resolve his disagreements with the co-ordinating committee at a general assembly of the MFA on 13 June. He proposed strengthening the powers of the prime minister over his colleagues, and holding presidential elections in the autumn. Popular endorsement, *à la* de Gaulle, which he was certain to get, would have immeasurably strengthened his hand over the MFA. The prime minister and his two PPD colleagues resigned in an effort to force the issue on 11 July, so bringing down the whole government.

Two days later, Spinola had lost his first major battle. An announcement was made that a new military command would be set up, the Operational Command for the Continent (COPCON) under Otelo de Carvalho. COPCON could in theory call on any unit in the country to enforce internal security, and Otelo was given, for good measure, command over the Lisbon military region, and was promoted from major to brigadier. Most telling of all, the new commander was appointed in a formal television ceremony, presided over by the president. Spinola may have been trying to split the radicals of the co-ordinating committee by luring the enigmatic major to his side; if he was, his tactic failed. The defence minister, Lieutenant-Colonel Firmino Miguel, a firm supporter of Spinola, was rejected as the president's choice for prime minister at a full meeting of the MFA. Instead, in a choice that was to prove more disastrous than even the radical soldiers can have supposed, Colonel Vasco Goncalves was nominated to the post. On 17 July, he was sworn in by a president who was powerless even to choose his own prime minister.

For two months more, the president struggled to free himself from the web in which he had so firmly entangled himself when he lent his prestige to the MFA. His one hope lay in mobilising the mass of officers who did not belong to the MFA. But by nature these were the non-political professional soldiers who had put up with fifty years of subservience to a right-wing minority in the armed forces, and were equally prepared to serve under a left-wing clique. The politically conscious right had been purged from the army after the 25 April coup, and a new group of officers unhappy with the trend of the new revolution had not yet had time to grow up. Too late General Spinola realised he was not in control. Too early he tried to do something about it. His constituency had not yet come into being.

Most of the officer class accepted the Socialist tenets now flung at them by their leaders and the Communist-dominated news media because Socialism was as meaningless to them as the vaguely corporative ideals of Salazarism had been to their fathers. Socialism was viewed by most officers as a rosy justification for acquiescing in the coup that had just taken place, the romantic expression of the army's new-found popularity. Only when the stampede towards economic disruption and state control began to yield disastrous results, and affect the officers' own interests, did they begin to question the new philosophy. And when they did, many of them rejected the democracy that Portugal had never seen, along with Socialism, as one of the failed innovations of the post-Caetano era.

The purges that began in all three services through the summer months of 1974 were never widespread enough to shake the non-political majority of officers into action. They affected, in general, only proclaimed conservatives; and the MFA was able to make major changes only in the navy, which was considerably more radical than the other branches. By late summer Spinola's efforts to mobilise the other branches became increasingly frenetic. In September he tried to summon a plenary meeting of the MFA to force the retirement of four leading members of the co-ordinating committee—Melo Antunes, Vasco Goncalves, Vitor Alves and Costa Martins. He failed.

And as he failed, so control of Portuguese policy ebbed further away from him. On 27 July Spinola, in a television broadcast, abandoned his previous insistence on gradual progress towards decolonisation. Guinea-Bissau and Mozambique, he announced, were to become independent with all possible speed, and Angola was to follow as soon as agreement could be patched up between its three independence movements. Yet Spinola was not above trying to outmanoeuvre his opponents over Angola, the richest of the Portuguese colonies. On 14 September he brought together the leaders of two of the independence movements in Angola, Jonas Savimbi of Unita and Holden Roberto of the National Front for the Liberation of Angola, together with President Mobutu of Zaire on the island of Sal in the Cape Verde group. The pro-Soviet Marxist leader of the third independence movement, Agostinho Neto, was left out, and in his place came the leader of a breakaway faction from within Neto's organisation, Daniel Chipenda.

Spinola's hope was to ease Neto's Popular Movement out of a share in Angola's future government, and so to protect the interests of the Portuguese settlers living there. Following the Sal meeting, Mobutu, who had established close relations with Spinola and had always backed the National Front, flew to Tanzania on 27 September to discuss the proposals that emerged with President Nyerere and President Kaunda of Zambia. But Spinola's plan was to be buried when he fell from power three days later, and so disappeared one of the few hopes, when the Popular Movement was still weak, of a peaceful settlement in Angola. Both Mario Soares, the Socialist foreign minister, and Rosa Coutinho, the Portuguese high commissioner in Angola, were furious at Spinola's secret initiative, and their disquiet was grist to the MFA co-ordinating committee's growing anti-Spinolism.

As Spinola struggled he allowed a campaign to be orchestrated by a flamboyant Portuguese architect, Jose de Almeida Araujo, the head of the self-styled Portuguese Liberal party, to win popular support. Posters appeared in the streets calling on Portugal's 'silent majority' to 'support the president and say no to the extremists'. On 22 September, he informed Admiral Rosa Coutinho that he would take personal charge of the process of decolonisation, then proceeding at breakneck speed.

Events came to a head when de Almeida arranged for Spinolist supporters, mainly ex-servicemen, to buy in advance the tickets to a charity bullfight being held in Lisbon on 26 September. The prime minister, Vasco Goncalves, was jeered on arrival at the bullring, whilst Spinola's appearance beside him was applauded. As the bullfight went on, Spinola was seen to be having an angry disagreement with Goncalves, who clearly blamed him for the demonstration. Outside, left-wing supporters of Goncalves gathered to protest against a proposed mass demonstration being organised by de Almeida in Spinola's support two days later. After several scuffles with police, the leftists showered stones on the crowd leaving the bullring. The clash left Goncalves and the radicals in no doubt that Spinola was planning something more than a peaceful demonstration on 28 September.

The plan, as agreed between Spinola and de Almeida, was relatively simple. Spinola would call a meeting with the MFA co-ordinating committee shortly before the rally, to discuss ways of lowering the Portuguese temperature. He would then place the leading radicals under arrest 'for their own protection' and go to welcome de Almeida's marchers—hoped to be at least 100,000—from the balcony of the presidential palace at Belem, in western Lisbon. The rally leaders would present the president with a list of demands, which he would promise to consider. He would assume emergency powers over the government, which he would attempt to confirm in a referendum in the near future. It was supposed that, presented with a *fait accompli*, most of the officers would stay loyal to the president. No real effort was made by Spinola to try to put together a subsidiary military operation, which would take over key points in the city the same day as the left-wing officers were arrested. That was to be left to de Almeida's civilians.

The co-ordinating committee was well aware that Spinola was trying to put together some such hasty, improvised plan. Their immediate concern was to prevent the mass rally taking place, which might lead to a confrontation between left-wing soldiers and conservative civilians, at which stage the soldiers might refuse to obey orders. The radical officers, though, were unaware of the arrest plan. Otelo de Carvalho took charge of the radicals' response, which consisted in alerting Communist and allied armed groups that his soldiers would not stop measures by armed militia groups to prevent the demonstration taking place; large quantities of arms were also distributed to the radicals' civilian allies. The Communist party leader, Alvaro Cunhal, took the added precaution of preparing a plane in case a quick getaway from the country became necessary. Communist barricades were set up on the approaches to Lisbon on the evening of 26 September.

On the morning of 27 September, Vasco Goncalves, after conferring with Alvaro Cunhal, went on the radio to attack his own information minister, Major Sanchez Osorio, a loyal supporter of Spinola. Goncalves denounced the major for giving an order to pull down the barricades, which Goncalves had himself signed. The prime minister was in turn rounded on for his action later in the day by Spinola: 'If minorities have the right to be heard, why should the same right not be recognised for the majority?' Spinola was all the more agitated at signs that his opponents knew his plans, and were preparing to outmanoeuvre him. By the evening he had decided to take the offensive. But by that time, Otelo and Goncalves had already prepared their own moves to follow up the cancellation of the silent majority rally with the arrests of prominent right-wingers, including General Kaulza de Arriaga, on a bogus plot charge.

Spinola ordered the Junta of National Salvation, the army chief of staff, General Costa Gomes, and some of his aides to Belem palace that night, then summoned his chief opponents, Otelo and Goncalves. Goncalves feigned a jovial manner, and attempted to shake hands with General Galvao de Melo. 'I do not speak with sons of bitches,' the right-wing general told him shortly, and the confrontation degenerated into a hopeless slanging match. Otelo, on his arrival, was told by Spinola that both he and the prime minister were to place themselves under the direct command of Costa Gomes as commander in chief, and of Spinola himself. Otelo was then instructed to telephone his subordinates with a string of orders that conflicted directly with his earlier orders to them to seize the radio stations and occupy key strategic posts. Otelo spoke at unusual speed to his subordinates, which aroused the suspicion at COPCON headquarters that he was under arrest, which, in effect, he indeed was. When he attempted to leave in the early hours of the morning, one of Spinola's staff officers prevented him from doing so.

Reports reaching Belem palace soon convinced Spinola that COPCON units were not carrying out the orders he had dictated to Otelo. The COPCON troops were staying put, and not dismantling the barricades. Worse, the army chief, General Costa Gomes, sensing the mood of the occasion, began one of those delicate exercises in political survival that were to earn him the title 'the cork'—no matter what, he would always bob about on top. He began to side with Otelo in the argument, and suggested that Spinola call off the demonstration so as not to provoke violence. Costa Gomes finally persuaded the president, whose hopes had been so naively founded on the irresistible strength of a mass popular demonstration, to release Otelo and Goncalves. Spinola at no stage tried to rally loyal units to his support against Otelo's COPCON detachments. He had neither prepared them for such a role, nor warned them in advance, and he knew that many non-aligned commanders did not see the danger of a left-wing takeover in such stark terms as he. Portuguese would not fight against Portuguese. He knew them too well.

At midday, as COPCON soldiers reinforced the Communist barricades, and turned back truckloads of right-wing demonstrators converging on Lisbon, Spinola issued a short communiqué:

> In view of the changed state of public order, which arose in the early hours of today, his excellency, the President of the Republic, considers it inappropriate that the rally announced for this afternoon in the Praca do Imperio should take place, in order to avoid possible confrontation.

The game was over. Portugal had taken its biggest step yet from authoritarianism of the right to authoritarianism of the left.

The prime minister's office quickly fabricated a story that Goncalves's life had been threatened by an unknown assassin who had hidden in an apartment with a telescopically sighted rifle across the road from his house. Subsequently, the apartment in question was found not even to overlook the prime minister's house, and the alleged assassination attempt was not referred to in the official account of the coup attempt published by the radicals in April 1975. An anti-fascist witch-hunt was set in motion, and de Almeida fled abroad to join the flotsam of circulating Portuguese exiles abroad. Otelo ordered a round-up of Caetano sympathisers and other right-wingers—including the former foreign minister, Franco Nogueira, and General Kaulza de Arriaga himself. But the arrests were curiously inadequate and indiscriminate, as if Otelo felt he had only to go through the motions of being a revolutionary. Spinola himself was charged with being the dupe of counter-revolutionary forces, but the radicals did not dare to force him out, for fear of precipitating a backlash among the non-political army officers who had failed to rally round him on 28 September.

Spinola's refusal to draw blood, though, meant that most officers were in complete ignorance of the showdown until after it was all over, and had never had the opportunity to take sides. Now all Spinola had to do was resign for them to lose not only the chance of rallying, but also the figurehead around which to rally. And a day and a half later, Spinola obliged the army radicals by resigning, on 30 September. A bitter speech denouncing Portugal's 'new slavery' was his last word to the Portuguese people from office. A month later he was retired from active service by a military edict which arbitrarily lowered the retiring age of generals to sixty-two (he was sixty-four).

4 The revolution devours its children

Spinola was succeeded as president by General Francisco da Costa Gomes, the army chief of staff, and his old superior under Caetano. A thin, mournful-looking man, his face always bore an expression of sad resignation towards the burdens that life seemed to have thrust upon him. With none of the panache of his predecessor, he was to bring a much more applied political mind to the game, but he seemed to have no constructive objective except to avoid tomorrow's bloodshed and stay in office. Compromises and temporary agreements that merely postponed the settling of scores, sometimes only to the next day, were the new president's stock in trade. Costa Gomes had backed Spinola against the conservative generals under the old dictatorship, and was not without political courage: he had had to pay the price of dismissal under Caetano. But once he had identified the interests of the country with his own position and the need to avoid spilling blood, he spared none of his considerable talent for political manoeuvre to pursue them. He seemed unaware that the longer the swing to the left was allowed to continue, the more violent the pent-up emotions of the right were likely to become.

From September until the elections of the following April, Portugal slid steadily down the slope towards a minority, left-wing military dictatorship. The MFA radicals, aware that the non-political centre of the army was wholly disorganised, grew bolder every day. Policy decisions in an already impotent cabinet were rammed down the throats of the increasingly unhappy non-Communist members, who knew that real power lay outside their grasp. The MFA grew franker about its intentions: at a press conference in London on 5 November, Vitor Alves confirmed that the army would act against an elected constituent assembly 'if the people pressed for it'. The MFA broadsheet, its 'bulletin', said much the same in an issue the same month: 'the MFA will have to guarantee that the constituent assembly is not only truly representative of the people, but also that the new constitution is imbued with the same progressive spirit as the MFA programme.' In other words, free elections yes, but only if you support our ideas. Right-wing officers were reorganised, reposted and purged, as autumn turned

to winter—but only in small numbers. The radicals dared not antagon-
ise the non-political bulk of the officer corps.

Shorn of right-wing leaders, only the intermittent self-doubts of
idealistic army Socialists existed to delay the inexorable path of revolution. The most prominent of these was the recently promoted General
Carlos Fabiao, the last governor of Portuguese Guinea and Portugal's
army chief of staff since the end of October. Fabiao embodied the
contradictions of an able professional soldier holding genuine democratic and Socialist ideals. The army beneath him was beginning to
disintegrate, as Communist and far-left ideologues converted soldiers
to ideals that were frankly anti-disciplinarian, and Fabiao knew at heart
that a professional army could not be run in this way. He knew that a
country could not stay idle and live off its reserves indefinitely—but he
could not yet bring himself to blame the Portuguese revolution for the
country's economic difficulties.

Fabiao was Portugal's Hamlet—undecided, caught between the two
stools of idealism and efficiency. He commanded greater support
amongst his brother officers than the MFA radicals, including Otelo,
but he was always perplexed. He had also been an associate, from
African days, of General Spinola, falling out with him eventually—
Fabiao considered the ex-president to have been the foil of reactionary
forces on 28 September. But he continued to admire Spinola as a
leader, and was more democratic than most of his colleagues. As he put
it in an interview with the author in December, which helped to reveal
some of the genuine confusion in MFA thinking that was bedevilling
Portugal at the time:

> The Armed Forces Movement will have attained its objective . . . on
> the day when the Portuguese nation is led by a democratic govern-
> ment freely elected by the people. From then on its action as the
> motor of April's revolution will have ended. The armed forces will
> subordinate themselves completely to the nation once sovereignty
> rests with the nation . . . once this expresses the popular will. In the
> meantime a complete subordination to the political authority will
> never become possible again because this would be a gross repetition
> of the mistakes of the past. The MFA's dissolution will be practically
> impossible because it is fundamentally the spirit which animated
> hundreds of young people . . . in the same ideals of peace, of justice,
> of renovation, of progress and freedom for all the Portuguese people.
> As long as its creators are alive, it is impossible to dissolve this spirit,
> which we want to perpetuate as the faithful guardian of the consti-
> tution and the people of our land.

Asked whether the MFA would ever act against the decisions of a
freely elected constituent assembly, Fabiao answered:

I've already been through the revolution of my life, and a revolution is a very serious occasion, which cannot be repeated often. It could be defeated and I wouldn't accept the defeat and would continue with my revolution which is, and will always be, that of April 1974. But this is possible during the revolutionary phase and as a consequence of a possible failure to fulfil the spirit of the programme of the MFA.

To act against a government which is legal and freely elected by the people, even if the people wanted it, would be to act against my convictions . . . if the people elected a government and then wanted to get rid of it, pressing me to do so, it would have to be because of one of the two following conditions were true: either the people had allowed themselves to be deceived into choosing wrongly, which would indicate political immaturity; or . . . I would be interpreting their wishes wrongly and would have allowed myself to be deceived by a clever but unrepresentative minority. In the second case, obviously . . . I would be acting against what I understood by democracy. In the first case I should take the same view because under such circumstances I would surely end up by falling into the sterile game of low politicking, of revolutions and counter-revolutions . . .

On the Communist party, Fabiao believed that

Communists interpret democracy in a different way from so-called Western societies. For them democracy only exists within the party itself, for Western societies in the plurality of parties. The Portuguese Communists accept the democratic game according to the Western view.

Fabiao considered the events of 28 September as 'a generalised popular explosion, showing that the Portuguese were not disposed to abdicate a freedom so long and anxiously awaited and finally achieved.'

Nevertheless, he was worried enough by the dangers posed to those freedoms to try and make the MFA co-ordinating committee more democratic, more representative at least of the army.

In November, Fabiao attempted to bring some control to bear on the co-ordinating committee. In a happy marriage between his own democratic ideals and his anxiety as to the then direction of the revolution, he tried to institutionalise the MFA: he convoked a general assembly, democratically representative of the whole Portuguese officer class, to which the co-ordinating committee would be responsible. On 6 December, Fabiao secured the first plenary meeting of the MFA's 400 officers since July, and, from the moderate tenor of the economic plan that emerged, he seemed to have checked the worst excesses of the move leftward. The co-ordinating committee would have to listen, after Fabiao began to organise a structure of officers' committees to elect delegates to the MFA's general assembly. The co-ordinating committee, from being a tiny left-wing minority dominating the larger minority of officers that made up the Armed Forces Movement, would now have to answer to all officers in the Portuguese armed forces.

Just how serious a challenge this would prove to the radicals became apparent in late February, when the first series of delegate election results became known. The non-political but distinctly conservative bulk of Portuguese officers, unprepared to fight the powers that were, was nevertheless prepared to vote against them. A swathe of radical candidates standing for election as delegates to the MFA general assembly, including Otelo de Carvalho and Vasco Goncalves, were defeated. The blow shook their prestige, although it did not affect their positions as members of the co-ordinating committee.

The votes came at a particularly discomfiting moment, after Otelo had cockily published a book in January belittling Spinola's role in the revolution of 25 April and accusing the ex-president of sneaking support for the old Caetano regime. The book also claimed that the general had wanted to call in South African or American troops in June to prevent Mozambique's independence. Spinola strongly rejected the attack in a statement published a week later. The following month the mass of Portuguese officers made it clear whose version they believed when they voted for known Spinolists in the MFA assembly elections.

As Otelo well knew, the elections were only the tip of an iceberg. In November, the first links had been established between clandestine right-wing organisations of ex-Salazarists outside Portugal, and those civilians and soldiers, particularly in the north, who were wondering how to check the current drift of events. Spinola himself knew about the outside organisations, but considered them too right-wing and too weak to provide a serious basis for an attempt to regain power. His real concern was to work within the army inside Portugal, and to gain the widespread support of democratic forces, who were by now seriously alarmed that the Communist party might be within throwing distance of gaining total control of the country.

Spinola fixed on Mario Soares, the Socialist party leader, as his obvious ally. For one thing, Soares had a clear charismatic appeal in the country. For another, he could hardly be denounced as a fascist. In February regular consultations were being held between intermediaries for Spinola and Soares. Popular Democratic leaders were also consulted. General Fabiao expressed to Soares his wish to restructure the co-ordinating committee in accordance with the officers' election results. Two of the more pragmatic radicals on the co-ordinating committee, Majors Melo Antunes and Vitor Alves, were becoming disillusioned with the impractical extremism of some of their wilder colleagues, and joined in the discussions. Even President Costa Gomes was indirectly consulted. Spinola proposed to hold back until the elections for a constituent assembly—scheduled for March—took place. These would either result in a crushing defeat for the Communist party—as unofficial opinion polls were then indicating—in which case the officers would have a good case for acting to make the government and co-ordinating committee truly representative of the popular will; Or the elections would be rigged or cancelled, in which case the moderates would have a pretext to act to restore the democracy promised in April 1974.

Spinola's plan formed the general basis for agreement. Towards the middle of February, however, the outlines of the plan and its probable adherents became known to the Communist party through supporters in its satellite party, the Portuguese Democratic Movement. In turn the Communists leaked their knowledge to MFA radicals, who decided to try and split what was potentially a lethal coalition against them. Goncalves, in prolonged discussions with President Costa Gomes, attempted to sow the seeds of discord by claiming that Spinola would be satisfied with nothing less than regaining the presidency.

Communist sympathisers on the left of the Socialist party likewise attempted to persuade their leadership that only Costa Gomes would be acceptable to the party as president. For Soares the argument was plausible enough. Whatever Spinola's intentions, he was clearly a conservative; whereas Costa Gomes, whilst avowing his commitment to democracy in Portugal, appeared to be a committed Socialist. Accordingly, towards the end of the month, Soares, Costa Gomes, Antunes, Alves and Fabiao adopted a common attitude to Spinola: after the radicals were defeated, Costa Gomes was to stay as president, and Spinola would have to content himself with the post of chief of staff.

Spinola felt himself betrayed. He had always gone out of his way to cultivate close relations with Soares, and Costa Gomes had previously assured him of his personal reluctance to take the post of president. Spinola felt himself bound by a historic mission as guarantor of Portuguese democracy. Worse, this kind of hedging might indicate that Soares himself had joined the ranks of those who would prefer to see Portugal under some form of dictatorial Socialism—much less extreme, of course, than under the present MFA leadership, but no less undemocratic for that. Spinola felt he had enough personal support in the armed forces to go ahead, make a coup succeed, and dictate the conditions for a return to democracy. But he must act soon, before Costa Gomes had time to rally dissident support to his side.

On 22 February, the northern military commander, Brigadier

Eurico Corvacho, thought by most officers to be a Communist party member, rang Otelo de Carvalho in Lisbon to say that he had information that a right-wing coup attempt would be made on 27 February. Corvacho said his informant was a double agent belonging to the extreme right-wing group then beginning to make a name for itself, the Portuguese Liberation Army, ELP. The coup would be aimed at two targets: air force planes would bomb the pro-Communist Light Artillery Regiment (RAL-I) in its barracks near Lisbon airport. Right-wing troops would also move in on the headquarters of the Republican National Guard at Carmo, and attempt to win the soldiers there to their side. Otelo took some precautions, but 27 February passed without incident. Corvacho thereupon telephoned to say that he thought that the coup had been postponed until 9 March.

The plans leaked by Corvacho were not dissimilar to the early operational planning of the pro-Spinola forces. The ex-president also intended to move in and take over radio stations. The planning centre for this coup would be the Tancos air force base, which contained paratroops loyal to Spinola and was commanded by Spinola's colleague, Colonel Rafael Durao. The other key units in the uprising were to be the commandos, commanded by another Spinolist, Colonel Almeida Bruno, the air force, under the right-wing General Mendes Dias, and the tanks stationed at Santarem under the command of Captain Salgueiro Maia. Spinola hoped that as soon as the coup was staged wavering supporters of President Costa Gomes, such as General Fabiao, and the political parties themselves, would bring their support to bear. Once again, he overestimated the political indignation of the bulk of the Portuguese officer corps, most of whom still did not want to get involved in politics if they could possibly help it. Spinola even had a 'shadow cabinet' in preparation, with Mario Soares as his preferred prime minister when he regained control.

But preparations for the coup were only half advanced when a leading ELP member, Lieutenant Nuno Barbeiri, announced at a meeting on 8 March, that a 'Lista de Matanca'—death list—of some 1500 leading right-wingers, including Spinola, had been drawn up. They were to be arrested and killed by the far left the following week. The rumour may have been a deliberate Communist provocation to get the right to show its hand too early; Corvacho's earlier talk of doubt agents suggests this, as does the second of his two dates for a possible uprising—9 March. Or it may have been an attempt by the extreme right to try and trip up Spinola. Both the extreme right and the Communists seemed to be agreeing at this stage on the need to do down the moderate General Spinola.

But the first that Spinola heard of the threat to his life came in a telephone call on the evening of 10 March, urging him to move north to Tancos without delay to avoid being killed. In a state of considerable confusion and haste, he made his escape from Lisbon. Says Otelo: 'Spinola was fooled; he had no idea what was going on. He had no real responsibility for it.' The ex-president arrived at the base, and agreed that the uprising must take place now or never. With Colonel Durao's agreement, at 10.45 A.M. 2 Harvard trainer propeller planes took off, accompanied by 3 helicopter gunships and 8 transport helicopters carrying 160 paratroopers. At 11.45 A.M. the convoy was spotted over Lisbon, and President Costa Gomes asked Otelo to send his COPCON troops into action. The security commander also ordered anti-aircraft guns to fire at the planes after they started bombing the RAL-I barracks at 12.00. The paratroops landed, took Lisbon airport and surrounded the RAL-I barracks. Another pro-Spinolist, General Durao, took control of the Republican National Guard barracks in Carmo. And a group of right-wing civilians managed to sabotage the commercial radio station, Radio Clube Portuguesa.

But other supposedly pro-Spinola units did not move. In despair, the ex-president tried to persuade his reluctant brother officers by telephone from Tancos. But General Mendes Dias kept his planes grounded. Colonel Bruno kept his soldiers in the barracks. And Captain Salgueira Maia's tanks stayed at Santarem. All three had been surprised by the swiftness of the decision to move and suspected that Spinola had fallen into a trap; they would not act.

Without wider support, the coup fell quickly apart. Surrounded by a hostile crowd, unwilling to spill blood, the paratroop commander outside RAL-I gave up after a few hours. At 2.00 p.m. General Durao surrendered at Carmo, and tried to escape from the scene. Captain Salgueiro Maia, in an attempt to display his loyalty to the MFA, flew to Tancos and demanded Spinola's surrender. The general sadly realised he had been let down, and with eighteen officers and his wife was allowed by Maia to escape in helicopters to Spain. The air force commander ordered that Spinola should not be pursued. After three days, the general with the monocle was expelled, and found political asylum in Brazil, on condition that he did not engage in political activity. The condition was to be far from respected.

The bungled coup of 11 March appeared to mark the end of moderate hopes in Portugal. Another wave of arrests swept up the implicated Spinolists. No hand was lifted by the majority of moderate officers to defend them, as Spinola appeared to have admitted his guilt by fleeing abroad. Monge, Bruno and several others were imprisoned, although another Spinolist, General Galvao de Melo, escaped arrest by giving himself up to the commander of the nearest military garrison to show he was not implicated. Galvao's position after the military coup of 25 April in charge of winding up the PIDE's operations is also thought to have played its part in keeping him at liberty: the PIDE files contained compromising material exposing how many of the officers now guiding the revolution had supported the old regime. Fabiao, Costa Gomes, Antunes and Alves kept their heads down and made no attempt to defend Spinola, so as to avoid being implicated in the coup attempt.

A foretaste of things to come was Otelo's press conference on the evening of 11 March in which he roundly attacked the American ambassador in Lisbon, Frank Carlucci, and said he could no longer guarantee his safety. The allegation that Carlucci was involved was unfounded, made on the spur of the moment and later apologised for, but it was typical of the triumphalism now indulged in by the radicals. They proceeded, in the succeeding days, to implement new and far-reaching nationalisation measures, scrapping the moderate economic plan they had drawn up in February. They replaced the entire elaborate 25 April power structure—Junta of National Salvation, Council of State, MFA co-ordinating committee—with an enlarged version of the co-ordinating committee, the Supreme Revolutionary Council, consisting entirely of left-wing military members.

So left-wing in fact, that the two radical socialists who only the autumn before appeared in the vanguard of the revolution—Majors Vitor Alves and Melo Antunes—were almost left off it as being too moderate. Only at the last moment were they reinstated at the insistence of Admiral Vitor Crespo, the Portuguese high commissioner in Mozambique, who was shortly returning to Lisbon with several thousand disciplined troops. The façade had been torn away: only a reshuffled provisional government was left to carry on the tenuous fiction that Portugal's rulers would like one day to see democracy installed. And the new provisional government contained more soldiers, and included members of the Communist-controlled Portuguese Democratic Movement for the first time. It was as unrepresentative as it was a sham.

Otelo and Goncalves moved equally quickly to stifle Fabiao's attempt to make the MFA more representative. 'Suspect' units—in practice a very large proportion of the Portuguese army—were debarred from holding delegate elections to the constituent assembly. The general assembly was made more 'representative' but less democratic by including selected delegates—mostly Communists—from the ranks of lieutenant, sergeant and private. And membership was firmly fixed to give the air force and navy together co-equal status with the army. Finally, three weeks after the uprising of 11 March, the Supreme Revolutionary Council put forward its own constitutional plan, which was to make a travesty of the idea that the elections due to be held in March—later deferred to April—would have any meaning at all.

Under the terms of the plan, military rule would be institutionalised

for a three- to five-year transitional period and all the major decisions
of the constituent assembly would have to be ratified by the MFA. The
political parties were told that unless they assented to these proposals,
they would suffer the same fate as the tiny Christian Democratic party
a few days earlier. The party had been dissolved after its leader, Major
Sanchez Osorio, who was implicated in the Spinola conspiracy, had
fled abroad. And so, in a televised ceremony at Belem palace on 11
April, one by one the party leaders—Mario Soares for the Socialists,
Sa Carneiro for the Popular Democrats, Freitas do Amaral for the
Centre Democrats, and an openly triumphant Alvaro Cunhal for the
Communists—filed past to sign the pact assenting to military control
over Portugal's future for an indefinite period. It looked like one of
those scenes from the 1930s when helpless Eastern European leaders
sadly signed away their countries to the brute force of Nazi Germany.

Yet, by finally coming into the open, the small minority military
government had exposed itself. The MFA radicals had eliminated only
the current leaders of the opposition in the armed forces, but not the
potential for opposition. They had detached the mass of officers from
any say in the decision-making process, which was to sow the seeds of
discontent when those officers began to want a say. Only purges, and
ruthless repression on a much wider scale could have consolidated the
radicals' hold on power in the army—and this they were unwilling and
unprepared to do because their power for the moment rested on bluff.
Their strength had never yet been challenged by force of arms, and
depended to a large extent on their opponents'—and the non-political
army officers'—unwillingness to shed Portuguese blood.

At the same time the radicals' conviction that their opponents had at
last been routed led to the beginnings of a debate between them about
the direction and type of Socialism suitable in Portugal. As most of the
radical officers had never given a moment's thought to the practical
application of the crude Marxism they had learnt in the African jungle,
as they were beset by personal rivalries, and as it became clearer that
they lacked any popular support, the divisions between them took very
little time to come out into the open.

5   The civilians struggle through

Portugal had only one organised political force after the fall of Caetano: the Communist party. Organised in underground cells, often very small, spread throughout the country, it was in a position to take immediate advantage of the confusion and the vacuum of authority after the fall of Caetano. Many of its operations, particularly in the north, were carried out under the aegis of the Portuguese Democratic Movement (MDP) an alliance the Communists had formed, chiefly at local level, with various anti-Caetano opposition groups, including Socialists, left-wing Catholics, and centre Liberals. Local authorities throughout the country had enjoyed some autonomy from central control under Salazar and Caetano, and the MDP claimed the right to take the reins of local authority power from their unrepresentative incumbents.

The Communist party was also strategically placed to take control of much of the press: for some time the party had followed a deliberate policy of infiltrating and controlling unofficial printers' unions in the national newspapers. The printing workers formed worker committees with sympathetic journalists on most of the national newspapers. In the early days many of the printers merely followed the lead taken by Communist union officials, and were later to rebel against their new masters. But by the summer of 1974, both in the press and broadcasting, the Communists had established a near-monopoly of news dissemination.

The trades unions were the third key area in which the Communist party established its immediate control. In many key industries, particularly around Lisbon, the Communist party already had activists among the labour force, and these began a rapid process of unionisation among their fellow workers. Party activists made the rounds of smaller firms around the country, setting up unions wherever they went. Trades union ideas were not to take a very firm root in many of these industries, and Communist penetration was fairly shallow. Where strikes took place, or workers' councils took over industries, these were often carried out against the wishes of Communist union convenors, or with their belated aquiescence. But to the other, more disorganised parties, the apparently monolithic Communist unions, and their economic power, presented a daunting prospect. For a long time afterwards the Communists' rivals in government were to view the party's inclusion in any coalition as indispensable: the Communists were thought to have the power to bring the country to a halt. The Communist unions were organised into a tightly-knit, hierarchical federation, called Intersindical, which fought for months to be acknowledged as the only legal union body, finally achieving its ambition in February 1975.

The Portuguese Communist party was the most hard-line, pro-Soviet in Western Europe. Its leader, Alvaro Cunhal, was an old-time *apparatchik*, who had spent more than eleven years in prison and then gone into exile abroad in Czechoslovakia in 1962. When his Spanish counterpart, Santiago Carrillo, roundly denounced the Soviet invasion of Czechoslovakia in 1968 from his exile in Paris, Cunhal as roundly approved. In fact, he supported every major Soviet initiative through the years in exile: if anything, he distrusted the liberalisation and deStalinisation begun by Khrushchev in 1956, and was cautiously identified with the Kremlin's hard-liners, men like the veteran party theoretician Mikhail Suslov, and the spokesman on foreign Communist parties, Boris Ponomarev. Cunhal's commitment was to gain power by compromise if necessary, by revolution if necessary. Tactical considerations alone governed his actions. The Soviet Union, during the first phase of the Portuguese revolution, was also clearly impressed by his chances of gaining power by climbing on to the radical military bandwagon, and gave him unqualified support. Not until Cunhal seemed on the point of failure, and the United States had unequivocally defined Portugal as a crucial sphere of interest, was the Soviet Union's support for the Portuguese Communist party called into question in the Kremlin.

On 30 April 1974, five days after the military coup, Alvaro Cunhal returned to his homeland. A crowd of about 3000 people greeted him at Lisbon's international airport, and he addressed them briefly but emotionally from an armoured troop carrier. It was the last sign of emotion the Portuguese were to remark in him for a long time. Small and slight, unimpressive physically, Cunhal makes up for it with a large distinctive face, huge black eyebrows and flowing white hair. When talking he fixes his bright sharp eyes on his listener, and lets pour with a flood of sharp, crisply delivered rhetoric, all of it carefully rehearsed, carefully calculated to say just as much as he wants to convey. For all the appearance of spontaneity, Cunhal is not a natural speaker, which on occasion leaves him at a disadvantage. His speeches are too prepared, too monotonously delivered in a nasal, almost academic, voice to arouse much enthusiasm even among his most stalwart supporters. Posed an unexpected question by an interviewer, he can sometimes be caught off balance, as when on 13 June 1975 he admitted in so many words to the Italian journalist Oriana Fallaci that he 'could not care less about elections'. Subsequent denials could not sidestep the fact that his words were recorded on the tape Miss Fallaci's secretary made of the interview.

Cunhal's immediate strategy was an attack on all fronts. His party had the media, the unions and the local authorities—it seemed logical that he would be able to convince the voters as well. In the army, the party had strategically placed supporters, such as Vasco Goncalves, and could get along happily, at least, to begin with, with the erratic radicalism of other MFA officers. As a party of order and discipline, the Communists were certain to prove more attractive to the armed forces than the other parties. The push was on to increase Communist support in the MFA, to appear economically responsible by, for example, controlling strikes, and to win votes through a saturation propaganda campaign.

The propaganda campaign had at least one effect: it discredited the right. Anything that was not at least Socialist was fascist, and fascism, support for the old regime, became a thing of shame, liable to be justifiably denounced by the local Communist group, or by the authorities themselves. The MFA obligingly banned one right-wing party after another—the National party, the Progressive party, the Liberal party—for fear that these could provide rallying points for some future right-wing challenge. And parties which were later supported by intimidated conservative voters moved leftwards, so as not to offend the country's military rulers, and also to pander to the new Socialist climate, which they thought would drive voters inevitably to the left in the coming months.

Although it was not realised at the time, the party that stood to gain most in electoral terms from the Communist strategy was the Socialist party. Fifty years of dictatorship had firmly imprinted on the Portuguese people the dangers of Communism. Communist rule, they felt, inevitably led to a dictatorship along Eastern European lines, far worse than anything endured under Salazar. Communism was an atheistic and Godless creed to a strongly Catholic people. But Socialism, whose virtues the Communists unwittingly proclaimed in every newspaper, broadcast, speech, tract and poster, was an altogether different matter. And no sooner had Mario Soares, the Socialist leader, reached Lisbon from Paris by train than he gave the 6000-strong welcoming crowd his firm commitment to a more attractive ideal still, democracy.

In its leader, the Portuguese Socialist party found itself doubly fortunate. Soares had charisma—his round, friendly face gave him immediate electoral appeal and made him the country's most recognisable figure after Spinola. And in his speechmaking, he had something that Cunhal lacked: a warmth and passion as the demagogic defender of socialism and democracy that for a while were to give him the air of an authentic Portuguese martyr, struggling against the forces of totalitarianism. Soares was also a first-rate political tactician. He had considerable defects as well. He combined a certain petulance of behaviour with indecisiveness, and would frequently allow his actions to be dictated by emotional rather than rational considerations. A host of mistakes were to be laid at his door. But the myth surrounding him did more to staunch what appeared to be the inexorable march of Communism than the reality. His jovial figure, applauded and recognised wherever he went, exchanging handshakes with those about him, became the symbol of the Portuguese freedom threatened by the small spare figure of Alvaro Cunhal, who never exposed himself to the public embrace, and went nowhere without a posse of forbidding bodyguards.

Soares had to lead a very diffuse party. Most of the opponents of Salazar who refused to go along with Stalinist Communism and had been lightly touched by Socialist ideals called themselves Socialists, joined the party after the coup, and used it as a label for whatever haphazard convictions they sought to impose on those about them. The party embraced everything from the reasoned faith in a mixed economy held by Salgado Zenha, the first minister of justice under the post-Caetano regime, to the left-wing extremism of those intent, in defiance of edicts from Communist unions, on strike action and workers' take-overs. Mario Soares was rosily optimistic about the chances of installing democracy in Portugal in April 1974, and his chief objective as party leader was simply to win widespread popular support. He was soon, though, to be locked in a much grimmer struggle to hold his party together and to collaborate with the MFA as long as the very smallest vestige of democratic hope survived in Portugal.

Further to the right, the political alignments were confused for a considerable period after the coup. The middle-class Liberal party, which had won seats in the national assembly in opposition to Caetano, but had withdrawn from the assembly in 1973 in protest against that institution's lack of power, only began to be reborn in a new guise—as the Popular Democratic party—in May. The party was led by one of the former Liberal leaders, Francisco Sa Carneiro, an aloof but respected young lawyer. His principal subordinate was Francisco Pinto Balsemao, the editor of the excellent weekly newspaper *Expresso*, which retained its editorial independence and rapidly passed from being Portugal's most left-wing publication under Caetano to being the country's most right-wing publication under the MFA. Balsemao, a smooth, nebulous talker, was more a salesman than a politician. His deputy on *Expresso*, Marcello Rebelo da Sousa, was also in the party hierarchy. A brilliant writer and clever manipulator, he was more devoted to the tricks of the political game than to its goals.

The PPD's chief concern was to try and win the support of all those frustrated by the lack of a significant right-wing party, whilst professing sufficiently Socialist ideals to assuage the prejudices of MFA leaders. So on the one hand the PPD and Socialist leaders welcomed the absence of competition from the right, and accepted the MFA's blanket charges of fascism as an excuse for suppressing right-wing parties. On the other they grew increasingly unhappy as they were driven to the left. PPD rhetoric became steadily less meaningful and more obscure as the party tried to distinguish itself from the Socialist party, while pandering to the MFA's revolutionary inclinations. 'Popular humanism' and 'social personalism' became the catch-phrases for a programme which, when eventually published at the end of the year, was to accept nationalisation on a very wide scale.

The PPD's decision to adopt a specifically Socialist approach, however general the terms in which it was couched, drove one group of potential sympathisers into forming their own party. Diogo Freitas do Amaral was a law professor at Lisbon university, and previously a pupil of Marcello Caetano. A tall, quiet, gentle man, he had an impressive fixity of purpose and an agile mind, which were to make him Portugal's best political performer on television. Freitas do Amaral was made a member of the council of state by Spinola, and together with an emotional but shrewd civil engineer turned journalist, Adelino Amaro da Costa, founded the Centre Democratic party (CDS). Its aim was to capture the large block of unrepresented voters on the right, and its programme favoured a mixed economy along Western European lines. The other party to survive on the right, among a host of stillborn and banned splinter groups, was the Christian Democratic party, led by a pro-Spinola officer, Major Sanchez Osorio. The Christian Democrats only emerged after Spinola's resignation in September, to enlist the support of the Church behind his ideals. But Church leaders were at that time acting highly cautiously, and came up with little money and less moral support. Osorio had an able political mind, but found it difficult to project his stiff military personality to a wider audience.

The parties passed their first few months of liberty attempting to set up a grass roots organisation. They were helped in their task by international supporters. For the Communist party, about $10 million a month was laundered through the Moscow Narodny bank in London. For the Socialists, money, advice or logistical support came variously from the West German Social Democratic party, the French Socialist party, and to a lesser extent, the Italian Socialist and British Labour parties. The PPD originally was thought to have connections with President Giscard d' Estaing's Independent Republicans in France. And organisational advice was given to the CDS by the British Conservative party.

Portugal's first provisional government, formed on 16 April 1974, included Communists, Popular Democrats, Socialists and Independents. At that stage, the Socialist party broadly supported the Communist party against the parties to the right, for example on the issues of nationalisation and speedy decolonisation. Mario Soares, who as foreign minister was broadly in charge of the negotiations for independence, was only dimly aware of the confusion that too rapid a colonial withdrawal would create. Nationalisation of banking and industry proceeded as fast as an unhappy General Spinola and prime minister Palma Carlos could allow. Soares's frequent travels abroad as foreign minister were widely criticised at home, and the Socialist party was derided for its absentee leader. But the trips had the effect, in a country whose previous rulers had done little travelling, chiefly for lack of invitations abroad, of implanting Soares's reputation as a world statesman in the Portuguese mind.

Cabinet dissensions led to the prime minister's resignation on 9 July, and the formation of a new government further to the left, but still containing PPD, Socialist and Communist ministers. The moderate party leaders still appeared confident, after Vasco Goncalves's appointment as prime minister, that the revolution would not abandon its original democratic promise. The new prime minister gave them little reason to fear. Except for a characteristic outburst on television against a newspaper which had lampooned his beer-drinking celebrations on becoming prime minister, the tone of his statements was reassuring. Indeed, the Socialist party was at that time chiefly preoccupied with the danger from the right, not the left. In an attack on one of the members of the Junta for National Salvation, General Galvao de Melo, who had remarked that Communism was worse than fascism, one of the then leaders of the Socialist left, Sottomayor Cardia, declared on 25 August, 'reaction is growing from day to day'.

It was an easy mistake to make. The Communist party, anxious to build up its electoral strength, had firmly committed itself to democratic pluralism, and was advocating a moderate economic course. Its daily newspaper, *Avante*, was considerably more restrained than many other Lisbon papers. The doubts of the army radicals about the virtues of a party system had not yet been openly expressed. Yet grassroots Socialists, and Soares himself, were already having their misgivings about Communist intentions. Both the PPD and the Socialist party withdrew formally from the MDP in June, alleging Communist manipulation. But the Communists, and the small minority of left-wing Catholics left behind, did not abandon their hold on local government.

Even after the events of 28 September, and Spinola's resignation, the Communist party did not abandon its caution. As late as December, Alvaro Cunhal told the author, 'we can continue to co-operate with the bourgeois parties for as long as is necessary to consolidate the freedom we won on 25 April. And we must co-operate afterwards.' Only the military guard was being cautiously lowered, as radicals on the co-ordinating committee began to talk of their watchdog role over the political process after the March elections. Yet the pressures on the democratic parties were being steadily increased below the surface. Banking employees, defying their management, froze the supply of political contributions to the PPD and CDS. Politicians from both those parties were scarcely ever allowed to appear on television. Attempts by the Socialists and PPD to found alternative trades union organisations met some success, but were in many cases met by open hostility, sometimes violent, from Intersindical members.

Worse still, a wave of violence began in November that was designed to drive the two right-of-centre parties, the CDS and Christian Democrats, out of action, and to intimidate voters into moving further to the left. The first outbreak was on 4 November, when the CDS attempted to hold a public meeting in the Sao Luis theatre in the centre of Lisbon. The building was beseiged on the outside by several hundred demonstrators armed with iron bars, bicycle chains and firearms. An inadequate contingent of police held them at bay for long enough for the meeting to be abandoned. The mob then marched to CDS headquarters, which it sacked, destroying furniture, equipment and files.

The Maoist group, the Movement for the Reorganisation of the Portuguese Proletariat (MRPP) claimed credit for the attack, denouncing the meeting as a 'counter-revolutionary provocation'. The Communist party piously expressed its regrets about what had happened. Such acts, said Octavio Pato, the party's number two, 'do not serve democratic forces which are interested in the process of democratisation, but on the contrary place obstacles in their way'. Yet Communist activists had been recognised among the demonstrators. For the government, President Costa Gomes expressed his regret over the incident. Two days later, the Oporto offices of the CDS were sacked and set on fire.

Attacks on the two parties were, in the initial stages, not as roundly condemned by the democratic parties as they might have been: the Socialists and PPD stood to gain from the absence of any effective contender on the right. But the first major break between Soares and the Communists was not slow in coming. Cunhal, growing more confident by the day, pressed in January 1975 for a law to stamp out what he saw as the growing Socialist threat to the Communist trades union monopoly. Bitterly resisted by the Socialist and Popular Democratic members of the cabinet, the law recognised Intersindical as the country's only legal trades union organisation and was only slightly watered down in its final form. Trades union officials should be elected, it said, without specifying the date or form of election. Soares and Sa Carneiro were overruled by the MFA radicals, who had the power, and could only watch in growing anxiety the slow burial of their democratic hopes. Soares's desultory participation in dissident military planning was ended by the attempted coup of 11 March, the lurch to the left, and a reshuffle of the provisional government.

11 March was to mark the highpoint of the drive towards left-wing dictatorship. The democratic parties, who had seen their short-lived freedoms relentlessly eroded over the previous nine months, were too dazed by the speed of the attacks upon them over the next month to make much resistance. The government, once again, was reshuffled; Soares was shifted from the foreign ministry to the ministry without portfolio; more military men and two ministers from the MDP were appointed, so effectively giving the Communists half the civilian posts in government. Real power was formally vested in the Supreme Revolutionary Council: the government's functions were described as 'executive.' The Christian Democratic party, together with the Maoist MRPP and a former guerrilla association, the PRP/BR, (People's Revolutionary Party/Revolutionary Brigades), were suspended from fighting the elections, an almost complete victory for the Communist party, which was worried by the possibility of losing votes to the extreme left. The remaining parties to the left of the Communists had been infiltrated and were firmly loyal to the Communists. It came as something of a surprise that the CDS was allowed to contest the elections at all, but CDS leaders were in London at the time of the attempted coup, and returned on hearing of it. Sanchez Osorio, the Christian Democratic leader, had disappeared on 11 March and re-emerged in Spain in April.

The last nails were hammered into democracy's coffin a month later. A plan was proposed at the end of March by the Supreme Revolutionary Council giving the MFA control of the government for a transitional period of three to five years, drafting the major outline of the new constitution, and giving the MFA the power to veto any decisions taken by the constituent assembly. The Socialists and the PPD ministers threatened resignation from the government if the measure was carried. A week's interminable discussion among members of the Supreme Revolutionary Council ended with the issuing of a final forty-eight-hour ultimatum to Soares and the PPD leaders: accept the plan or be banned from fighting the elections.

The democratic parties' resistance collapsed after the ultimatum: for them the coming elections were the last straw they had to clutch, an opportunity to show that they had the support of the people, and an opportunity to make the MFA radicals aware of the unpopularity of the Communist party in the country. After signing the pact on 11 April, Soares was almost unreservedly pessimistic.

For a while it was touch and go whether the elections would take place at all. The MFA's own opinion poll revealed that the Communist party stood to win at most about 15 per cent of the votes, with the rest going almost entirely to the democratic parties—the Socialists, PPD and CDS—who had persistently, if unsuccessfully, tried to obstruct the course of revolution. But for the first time the divisions between the MFA radicals began to surface. Vasco Goncalves argued for the postponement of the elections, as indeed Alvaro Cunhal was privately demanding, on the argument that the Portuguese people were insufficiently prepared for democracy. The three weakened soldier-ideologists —Vitor Alves, Melo Antunes and Vitor Crespo—argued that the elections must take place if the original programme of the MFA (which promised elections within the year) was not to lose all public credibility. Their argument carried some weight with those non-aligned radicals, particularly Otelo, who were still wedded to the illusion that the soldiers were popular.

Increasingly Otelo was coming round to the view that the MFA could not afford to take sides in the party political debate. By backing the Communists, he felt, the MFA was endangering its affinity with the people, which could only last as long as it took an above-the-battle stance. The Communist party was, Otelo accepted, still the most revolutionary of the larger parties, and still the MFA's most useful ally; but it should not be allowed to gain a degree of power that was not rightly its own. Even the criticisms levelled by the foreign press against the Communist party were beginning to have their effect on Otelo and other non-committed army radicals. They were determined to show that the Portuguese revolution was different, was being led along their own idealistic path, and that they were not acting as Communist party pawns. Besides which, there might even be something in the foreign view that the Communist party would one day bid for the MFA's own power. Lastly, if the opinion polls were right, there was the danger that the MFA could be linking itself too closely with a falling, unpopular star, and that some of the Communist unpopularity might rub off on the army.

Otelo was beginning to accept that an election might be useful in assuaging foreign fears, and in cutting the Communists down to size. He was also beginning to see that his best allies were not the armed activists of the Communist party, but the supporters of the extreme-left parties, who were more truly revolutionary, were less susceptible to accusations of Soviet influence, and would never be in a position to contest MFA power.

The challenge to the Communists came, when it did, from an unexpected quarter: Portugal's high commissioner in Angola. Admiral Rosa Coutinho had recently returned to Portugal; he had firmly supported the then weaker, Moscow-backed Popular Movement for the Liberation of Angola (MPLA). By allowing the MPLA immediate access to strategic power in the capital, Luanda, he had created the basis for civil war against the other independence movements, and an eventual victory for the Marxists. He had also earned himself the undying hatred of the white community in Angola. On all previous and subsequent occasions he was to support the Communist party as faithfully as Vasco Goncalves had. But probably out of a mistaken assessment of his own importance on his return to Portugal, he stayed firmly out of Cunhal's orbit. Rosa Coutinho was ambitious, and wanted to replace Vasco Goncalves, whose defects of temperament were beginning to be apparent to even the most hard-line MFA members. The 'Red Admiral', as Spinola called him, thought he had a Soviet imprimatur to lead a stable, radical military regime which would give less offence to the United States than an outright Communist dictatorship based on a Cunhal-Goncalves axis.

Rosa Coutinho's first move in his assault on the office of prime minister was an agreement with Otelo de Carvalho that the elections must be held, so undercutting Goncalves's open alliance with the Communists. The results, whatever they were, would not affect the balance of power in Portugal anyway. As Coutinho told the author on 21 April, 'What do we care if the bourgeois parties win the elections? We have the power in our hands anyway.' Rosa Coutinho's second move was to fly a kite: he proposed that a single political party representing the revolutionary spirit of the MFA might be founded after the elections, which would eventually replace the existing 'divisive' political parties. He did not in so many words say that Portugal would be turned into a one-party state, but the implication was clearly there.

The proposal to go ahead with the elections was backed by the moderates and non-Communist radicals; even the loyalties of the pro-Communist group were split between Rosa Coutinho and Vasco Goncalves. The pro-Communist information minister, Commander Correia Jesuino, for example, voted with Coutinho, although he was later to veer back towards supporting the prime minister. The second proposal, to set up the MFA's own party, was hotly contested, naturally, by the moderate Antunes group, but also by the Communist officers: a political party already existed, they argued, that embodied the ideals of the MFA: the Communist party.

Goncalves too, aware of the danger to his position, set his own supporters in motion. The army's fifth division had been given the task of acting as an agitprop section, and mounting a campaign for 'cultural dynamisation' to spread the revolution through the Portuguese countryside. The unit was commanded by a loyal Goncalves supporter, Lieutenant Ramiro Correia. A small, fanatical, intense young man, Correia had been put in charge of a preliminary investigation into the facts surrounding the abortive coups of 28 September and 11 March. It was darkly hinted by Goncalves and Correia that the report would go very deep into the origins of both coups unless the MFA single-party proposal was dropped. Uncommitted officers like General Fabiao, who had been allegedly involved in the preparation for the March coup, got the message and switched away from supporting Coutinho to supporting Goncalves instead. As Rosa Coutinho became increasingly isolated, even Otelo moved away from supporting an idea with which he strongly sympathised, and two days before the election the Admiral quietly buried his plan: it was, he said, only 'a proposal for a coalition of the existing parties behind the MFA after the elections'. The same day, the preliminary report on the two coup attempts was published, containing most of the names of people already accused.

An interview given to the author by Alvaro Cunhal at about this time gives an idea of his view of the political in-fighting, as well as his bouncy over-confidence that he was on top of the revolution. He was opposed to the idea of the MFA creating a single party, he said, because:

> The MFA would lose its independence in relation to the parties, which is an essential part of its role in the revolutionary process . . . [The Communist party] firmly co-operates with the MFA in the context of an alliance between the people and the armed forces: If the elections were held in normal conditons, they would confirm the support of the people for the present democratic situation and the wide mass base of the Communist party.

The Communists, he thought, could get 19 per cent of the vote.

There was no danger of a reactionary comeback, Cunhal thought:

> Reaction has lost power in the armed forces. The defeat of the counter-revolutionary coups of 28 September 1974 and 11 March had as a consequence the removal of reactionary officers from the important positions they occupied. I think the MFA was never stronger than it is now. I am confident that if a reaction attempts a new coup, it will again be defeated and will pay an even higher price than on previous attempts.

So the elections went ahead. MFA leaders did their best to belittle their importance: on 3 April Commander Jesuino dismissed them as 'primarily a pedagogical exercise so as to provide a political panorama of the country'. For technical reasons the election date was moved on a month from its scheduled date to the anniversary of the coup the year before, 25 April.

Of the four main contestants, the CDS had been driven virtually underground by the intimidatory campaign mounted against it, and the party held only a few public meetings in the last two weeks at selected strongholds in the north. Yet the month of political campaigning by the others—the PPD, Socialists and the Communists—caught the imagination of many Portuguese. They had never experienced the election circus of public meetings, party broadcasts on television, and the mass of journalists—some 600 on election day—that converged on Lisbon from every quarter. And not even the damaging comments of MFA leaders could extinguish the flame of hope among the people. All meaning had been robbed from the elections by the military save the one they could not control—their symbolic value for the democratic aspirations of a people that had been deprived of both symbol and substance for over fifty years.

The Socialists made most of the running from the start of the campaign. Soares had become identified with the attempt to stop the country succumbing to a new dictatorship, and he criss-crossed the country indefatigably. He was greeted by huge crowds shouting the slogan that summed up his own thinking, '*Socialismo Si, Ditadura Nao!*' Soares's speeches were radical enough—attacks on monopoly capitalism, *latifundistas*, calls for nationalisation and worker solidarity—but they inevitably ended with appeals for democracy in the trades unions and in the local authorities. He fiercely warned of the threat of dictatorship from an unnamed source—and everyone knew that he was not talking about the right.

Soares would usually approach the podium to speak from a position in the crowd itself, unguarded, vulnerable to attack, but clearly in contact with the people. In the last week of the campaign he ventured down to Beja in the south, considered the Communists' capital city, where Cunhal had once said Soares would never dare to come. A cheering crowd of 10,000 people filled the bullring to hear him, with not a Communist in sight: he was to poll half of Beja's vote in the election five days later. 'It is not important that we have no immediate power to govern,' he told the author on that occasion. 'It is important that we have the kind of support you have seen here for yourself.'

The PPD played the campaign in a lower key in Lisbon and the south but campaigned vigorously in the north. Their leader, Sa Carneiro, had fallen seriously ill a month earlier, and was being treated in London, so that the bulk of campaigning fell on the shoulders of Francisco Balsemao, Marcello Rebelo da Sousa, and Magalhaes Mota, a minister in the provisional government. The party offered the only alternative to Socialism of one sort or another, but it had moved so far to the left, and so obscured its message, that it had difficulty in establishing an identity: it had no single popular leader. Nevertheless, widespread support from the Church at a parish level, as well as a considerable hostility towards all forms of Socialism among northern smallholders, gave the party a considerable popular base.

That base only began to be threatened in certain areas when the CDS began a small programme of popular meetings, featuring Freitas do Amaral, Amaro da Costa, and the Centre Democratic independent candidate for Viseu, Spinola's old aide, General Galvao de Melo. Galvao was the only politician who attacked Communism in so many words, and who criticised the MFA. Soares, for example would instead always unconvincingly end his speeches with a raggedly cheered '*O Povo esta com o MFA*'—'The people are with the MFA'. When local Communists cut electricity cables and blacked out a CDS meeting in Viseu, Galvao led thousands of supporters into a song, as rioters demonstrated outside. But the CDS campaign was too late to have any but a local effect.

The Communists always had a crowd. They were not as large as Socialist crowds, but quite as enthusiastic, despite their leader's aloof style of oratory. But they were mostly the same crowd: an enormously efficient organisation commandeered some forty buses to carry in supporters from outside wherever local organisers thought the stadium was in danger of not being filled. At two eve of poll meetings on successive nights, the Socialists and Communists rallied their supporters to Lisbon's First of May stadium. Some 50,000 Socialists came to hear Soares and watch him tussle with photographers, who kept getting in his way. The crowds waved its seas of banners in wild approval at his ever-hoarser oratory. Some 40,000 Communists came the following day to hear Cunhal attack Galvao de Melo, and watch his strong-arm men eject two Belgian television cameramen who had inadvertently moved too close to the assassination-conscious leader (an ex-PIDE agent was recognised among Alvaro Cunhal's bodyguards). But long rows of buses were to be seen outside Cunhal's rally where none had been seen outside Soares's.

To the last, many observers feared the poll might be rigged: counting was to be done by those same members of the MDP who had taken over the local authorities after the previous year's military coup. There was also the danger that widespread rioting by Communists outside polling stations would deter voters from going to the polls. Members of the Fifth Division, criss-crossing the country under Ramiro Correia's orders, advised anti-Communist voters to cross out the word Communist from their ballot papers, so spoiling their vote. The Communist party abandoned its plan for demonstrations, however, on learning that Otelo had put COPCON troops on alert to ensure that the elections would pass off without incident. Otelo also lent his support to an initiative of Coutinho's, which was transmitted to the nation on 23 April. Voters were advised by the information minister, Correia Jesuino, to cast blank ballots as a token of support for the MFA.

The idea backfired disastrously. On a balmy spring day 93 per cent of the Portuguese people went to the polls, and just 7 per cent of those cast blank ballots. The vote for the major parties was: Socialists 38 per cent, PPD 26 per cent, Communists 13 per cent, CDS 8 per cent, MDP 4 per cent. A few irregularities took place in the south, but otherwise the poll and counting, which were observed by representatives of all parties, passed off peacefully enough.

The PPD won a little more than the pollsters had predicted, the CDS a little less, but otherwise the vote went much as expected. The democratic parties had roundly trounced the Communist party. But that was not how the MFA saw it: a chastened Jesuino told journalists the following day that an absolute majority had been cast for Socialism, and so, indirectly for the MFA. 'Political elections' Jesuino went on,

> do not change governments. The government is chosen to have a maximum degree of operational effectiveness and this government has worked very well: all its decisions have been unanimous . . . The political parties must now begin to respond to the will of the people as expressed through the Armed Forces Movement.

The triumphant democratic parties had few illusions that their revolutionary rulers would be influenced by the electorate's choice. Mario Soares told the author that the elections were important not because they would give his victorious party any power, 'but because they give us a platform'. Other politicians resigned themselves to months of political struggle between the country's extremist soldiers. Said one: 'We are faced by a choice between a military dictatorship controlled by the Communists, and a radical military dictatorship without them. We prefer the second.'

Yet, although none of the combatants realised it, the elections were to be the major turning point in Portugal's struggle for liberty. They were to give the democratic parties not only the legitimate claim that they commanded the support of the overwhelming majority of Portuguese, but also the courage to pit their massive civilian strength against the brute force of the soldier radicals. In the end, the power of civilian protest proved more powerful than the vaunted firepower of the soldier radicals. As Otelo de Carvalho later told the author: 'In retrospect, our biggest single mistake was to have allowed the elections to go ahead. Our downfall can be traced from then.'

6 Pandora's box

When the captains took control of Portugal in April 1974, there were more than 1 million Portuguese—of the country's 10 million nationals —living and working abroad. They sent back £400 million in remittances every year to their families, because there was so little chance of finding work in their native country. Salazar's monetary policies had kept the economy stagnant, and had kept many Portuguese underemployed, until the African wars forced the government to raise taxes, expand the money supply and allow prices to rise. Price rises increased militancy among Portugal's normally tame labour force, and increased administrative costs, so that the money going into industrial investment fell to the lowest level in Western Europe.

The government, in a bid to curb economic discontent and boost the economy, relaxed its protectionist controls against foreign investment in the early 1960s. Tourism, agriculture and industry were in fact considerably boosted as foreign companies took advantage of Portugal's still extremely low labour costs, and proximity to European markets, to expand their operations. Between 1963 and 1970 real wages in Portugal rose by more than a quarter.

By the early 1970s the beginning of a rise in world commodity prices, as well as the rapidly accelerating cost of Portugal's African wars, forced Caetano's government to throw Salazar's monetary restraint to the winds. In 1971, prices were up by some 12 per cent, and increased again by about the same the following year. The clandestine Communist Party, which until then had had next to no support among industrial workers, was able to take advantage of the sudden brake on workers' rising living standards, and on May Day 1972 organised a succession of ill-attended strikes, a practically unheard of act of defiance in Portugal.

The government, trapped by its expenditure in Africa, had no alternative but to try to defuse the economic situation by easing credit. But Portugal's large and lazy monopolies were unwilling to expand, and its timid smaller industrialists were in no position to. When the monetarist chains were taken off, the Portuguese economy, like a prisoner who had been chained for fifty years, did not know how to walk. Easier credit just fed inflation, as the banks lent to the bigger firms to meet the cost of wage rises. By the first three months of 1974, inflation stood at an annual rate of 63 per cent. Strikes and stoppages were on the increase, and the large Leiria engineering plant in Lisbon was halted by a three-week strike in March 1974. The economy, in short, was getting out of control.

But if Caetano was hardly conspicuous by his success, his successors proved nothing short of disastrous. The April coup itself was orderly, and did little to frighten foreign investors. But in those first, uncertain days of freedom both Spinola and the MFA took time to adjust to economic realities. When they did, they disagreed, and for almost two years the economy became the plaything of political forces, as the resources built on so much Portuguese sweat by Salazar were squandered away. The old dictator had amassed a fortune by his miserly methods; and his sons, to whom he had never entrusted his money for a moment, were to blow it all away.

What happened to the Portuguese economy over the next nineteen months reads like a cautionary tale against the sudden imposition of dogmatic revolutionary economic doctrines on a sick economy. Industrial unrest led to a falling off in private investment, and the concession of still more inflationary wage rises. Ill-considered and piecemeal nationalisations turned investment into a negligible trickle, and channelled much of it abroad: foreign investors stopped investing, domestic ones smuggled their money out of the country. Nationalisations were increased as fewer private companies found the capital necessary to meet the rising costs of labour and raw materials, and the government had to step in to prevent unemployment. Workers' takeovers and chronic worker indiscipline also drove private firms out of business, and forced the government to come to their financial rescue. In order to meet the bills, the government expanded the money supply. Investment confidence further declined as inflation rose more quickly. The price of exports rose and the trade gap increased.

Inflation was only prevented from reaching prohibitive levels because the government sold off sufficient quantities of foreign exchange to maintain the value of the currency, so keeping import prices down to reasonable levels. But that meant that the price of imported goods fell in relation to the price of domestic products, and consumers channelled their new-found spending power into imports: which just widened the trade gap still further, and forced the government to dip further into its foreign exchange reserves. The country was being sucked into a vicious whirlpool of economic decline that would only end when reserves were exhausted. Profligate economic irresponsibility by a group of soldier rulers applying Marxist economic analysis brought Portugal to a state of economic near-anarchy, which almost brought most Portuguese to the edge of poverty and starvation.

Strangely enough, the Communist party was the chief force for industrial moderation in the months immediately following the coup.

Avelino Goncalves, a Communist trades union leader, was appointed minister of labour, and immediately tried to calm demands from more militant Communists to establish 6000 escudos (about $170) as the national minimum wage. On 6 May, just a fortnight after the military coup, a strike paralysed the huge Lisnave shipyard just south of the Tagus. But officials from the Communist party persuaded strikers to go back and negotiate. The Communist trade union organisation, Inter-sindical, occupied the offices of the Salazar regime's official union organisation, called, with a fascist flourish, the National Federation of Joy at Work (FNAT).

But Intersindical was far from controlling its regional branches. On 15 May, 8000 Lisnave workers occupied the shipyards. By the end of the month, some 200,000 people—in electronics, banking, printing, chemicals, textiles and other trades—had gone on strike, and worse was to follow. On 17 June, a 35,000-strong postal workers' strike was angrily denounced by the Communist party, which accused the strikers of helping 'fascism and reaction'. Such support was enough for Spinola to threaten the use of the army to break the strike. And shortly after-wards the strikers backed down. By July the minister of labour (Avelino Goncalves had been replaced by an equally pro-Communist officer, Costa Martins) used COPCON troops to reoccupy the plant of a large American company, Timex, taken over by the workers; the factory was restored to the owners.

The Communist party had good reason for its tactical quiescence. From the first, Alvaro Cunhal had pinned his party's chances on close co-operation with the MFA. His primary objective was to keep power in the hands of the army revolutionaries, in co-operation with the Communists. Discipline therefore had to be maintained, the Com-munists must be seen as the faithful tools of MFA policy. Secondly, Cunhal badly needed to establish monopoly control over the trades union movement. There was a danger—and Cunhal was slow to see it—that the Communists would gain scant support in a general election. Their original credentials to form part of the government, their sup-posedly mass support among Portuguese workers, might therefore have to become their continuing claim to government. Cunhal was alarmed enough by signs that union militancy might get out of his control to feel the need for the MFA to back up his claims to union hegemony.

He was equally alarmed by the attempts of other parties—in parti-cular the Socialists—to break Intersindical's clandestine monopoly of Portuguese trades unions. As a leading Socialist, Sottomayor Cardia, told the author in November 1974. 'Our tactic is to create a trades union movement to rival that of the Communists. Then we can dispose of their services in government.' Sure enough, the MFA's, and the Communists', firm line against industrial action drove a number of more militant unions even further to the extreme left, and drove others into joining the much more loosely disciplined Socialist party. Cunhal faced a dilemma: if he supported the militants, he would come into conflict with the armed forces; if he supported the armed forces, he risked losing the militants. In the event, he opted for the armed forces in the hope that they would seize on his party with relief as a stick for beating rebellious unions and the Communists' industrial rivals. The Communist leader very nearly succeeded. On 19 January, the government supported the new law granting a union monopoly to Inter-sindical.

Communist and government hostility to union militancy markedly reduced strikes in the second half of 1974, although wage rises approved by the government were large enough to add an inflationary twist, and plunge many Portuguese firms into a serious liquidity crisis. The government shrank from outright nationalisation, though, for a surprisingly long time after Spinola had fallen from power in September 1974. From November until January the following year, the MFA leaders debated an economic plan that would finally cut through the soldiers' muddles and disagreements. The architect of the plan was Major Melo Antunes, whose previously radical views had considerably mellowed in the face of Portugal's economic predicament.

Antunes was to cling to his Socialist objectives; but his thinking had been much influenced by an OECD report the previous summer, which proclaimed: 'the serious risk of a wages–prices explosion . . . is the major policy issue at present'. Antunes proposed setting up a national cost-of-living council containing representatives of management, unions and government, and incorporating a prices and incomes commission which would seek to contain wage settlements. Antunes was also working on the basis of a sobering economic end-of-the-year assessment by the budgetary authorities. The 1974 balance of payments deficit was estimated at $500 million, and the rate of price inflation at 18·1 per cent over the year. As the Banco Totta e Acores put it, 'As long as the rate of growth of salaries continues to outstrip that of prices and productivity, the external balance will remain firmly in deficit, as in the United Kingdom.' Antunes's proposals seemed to meet the problem.

Nor did the other provisions of his economic plan live up to the revolutionary rhetoric of the soldiers in power. A 51 per cent state holding was proposed in the mining industry, the extraction of oil, gas and petrochemicals, steel, the Sines Development complex in southern Portugal, tobacco, arms munitions and electricity. Anti-trust legislation was proposed to do away with the monopolies that had plagued private enterprise under Salazar, and state intervention was considered a possibility in the metal working, fertiliser and milling industries. But the programme fell far short of giving the state the degree of control urged by, for example, Otelo de Carvalho and Vasco Goncalves; and in the field of land reform it proposed only to take over acreage that had been left idle. The government proposed a public investment programme, but also intended to stimulate medium and small-sized enterprises, and guarantee the security of foreign investment. Income tax was to be raised, and taxes on capital gains, gifts, estates and non-distributed profits were proposed; but these measures were being introduced into a taxation vacuum, and were conservative by comparison with most of the tax legislation then operating in Western Europe.

Antunes's plan, although vague on details, might just have worked; Portugal's economy was in a bad but salvageable shape. But the man whom Spinola had once described as a Communist was not to stay in the driving seat for long. The failure of the attempted coup on 11 March opened the sluice gates for a revolutionary torrent which swept away the Antunes proposals and very nearly unseated the pragmatic major himself from a post on the Supreme Revolutionary Council. The banks were in the vanguard of the extremist cavalcade. The powerful Communist bank unions in Portugal's fourteen domestic-owned banks, joined by a few workers who had the temerity to belong to groups further to the left, took immediate advantage of the hysterical anti-fascist climate surrounding the aborted coup to close the banks on 11 March, and refused to reopen until control of the banks was handed over to workers' committees. On 14 March Vasco Goncalves approved their decision in an announcement declaring banks and insurance companies nationalised. The takeover was, he said, 'The first and decisive step towards implementing the anti-monopolistic principles embodied in the country's social and economic programme.'

In fact, the bank takeover was far from being the spontaneous worker movement then portrayed by the government. With almost clockwork precision, local Communist cadres had installed their leaders in managerial positions. In those branches where no Communist bank unions existed, managers were moved in from other branches. Among many groups of bank workers, the takeover proved highly unpopular. Employees were henceforth officially described as civil servants, who traditionally earned less than bank workers. And in the north nationalisation often meant the installation of Intersindical officials previously unconnected with banking as managers.

Workers' takeovers spread through Portugal the following month like a rash. In some cases, particularly in smaller firms, these were spontaneous. In most they were orchestrated at the Intersindical head office in Lisbon. The government happily yielded to the trend. On 15 April the most far-reaching nationalisation measures yet were announced by Portugal's military rulers. The government decided to take over fourteen electrical firms, the Portuguese railway company, the National Navigation company, the Portuguese company for Sea Transport, the Portuguese airline TAP, the oil companies—Sacor, Petrosul, Sonap, Cidal—and the Portuguese share in the multinational Soponata, and National Steel.

The green light was also given to the land seizures that were to become a prime focus for controversy over the coming months: all non-irrigated estates of over 500 hectares (1250 acres) and all irrigated estates of over 50 hectares (125 acres) were to be expropriated and distributed among peasants and farm-workers on the land. The proposed limits on land-holding were ludicrously low by any standards of efficient farm production. They were primarily decided by Portugal's own experience of land-holding, which was divided between large, inefficiently run estates in the south, and tiny, uneconomic estates in the north. The government assumed that the break-up of the large estates would be popular among the smallholders of the north. It wasn't: as takeovers became more and more indiscriminate, increasingly illegal, and spread further north, the smallholders were to marshal their forces in an all-out fight to resist the agrarian laws.

At the same cabinet meeting, the revolutionary government's new economic strategy, such as it was, became obvious. The government proposed to tackle the balance of payments problem by protectionist measures against 'superfluous goods'. At the same time, it decided to subsidise an extensive list of essential goods until the end of the year: bread, meat, milk, sugar, olive oil, flour, chicken, codfish and margarine. Subsidies were also proposed to lower the price of butter and peanut oil. More vaguely, the government gave notice of a national employment programme to combat unemployment, although how the government proposed to achieve this after the crippling blows it had just dealt private industry was not so clear. In fact the programme was paid for by a further expansion of the money supply, which could only add to the inflation that had already priced Portuguese exports out of foreign markets. And the government was even at that stage considering a boost in the national minimum wage—which had been increased in May by 21 per cent—as well as a host of social security laws which would impose stiff rates of contributions on employers.

At a press conference a week before the economic measures were announced, Vasco Goncalves appeared to pin some faith in hopes of aid from overseas. His labour minister, Costa Martins, had just returned from a trip to Moscow, where he claimed to have secured the promise of considerable economic aid. But the Kremlin was following a more ambiguous policy. The Russians needed more evidence that Portugal was securely in their camp before rushing in to subsidise a bankrupt economy on the scale of their other Western dependency, Cuba. And the Soviet economy could ill-afford another annual drain of the same kind. Russian officials privately advised Martins that they were willing to give; but Portugal should first attempt to secure economic relief from Western countries. The Russians belittled the political influence that Western countries could exercise through such trade.

Partly pandering to a domestic lobby, and partly to convince the Russians that Portugal had few hopes of viable Western support, Goncalves at his press conference denounced unspecified threats of 'economic sabotage' by Western governments. The prime minister attacked the chairman of the West German Bundestag, Herr Von Hasel, who had remarked that conditions in Portugal were not suitable for foreign investment. Goncalves also complained, again without citing details, that some individual firms had pulled out 'with no reason'.

But the truth was that the government's policies, and political instablility, made conditions unsuitable for any kind of investment. Industrial production in 1974 had fallen by one-fifth. Receipts from tourism had gone down by one-third. Unemployment had climbed to 200,000, some 8 per cent of Portugal's already underemployed work force. And in mid-April, Alvaro Cunhal, with the quiet satisfaction of an animal stalking his prey, estimated that about 300 companies, containing 200,000 employees, were then on the brink of bankruptcy. The answer for Cunhal and Goncalves was, of course, a government takeover. To stave off the evil day, companies had been borrowing on international money markets, paying a full 5 per cent additional premium for political risk. But the process of socialisation through bankruptcy had already begun. In just ten days between 6 May and 16 May, forty-nine firms were nationalised.

Not all the economic signals from NATO countries were negative. The Dutch government, which favoured a substantial EEC grant to Portugal, made a small contribution of its own of about $30,000 in April. The president of the EEC council of ministers visited Portugal on 2 June, and assured the government of EEC support if the country developed democratic institutions. The Americans offered Portugal a small loan of $20 million in December 1975. But most foreign lenders were cautious, waiting to see where the country's slapdash economic experiments would lead.

But as the year wore on the government and its Communist allies were too anxious not to lose the support of union militants to do much to control their increasingly destructive activities. The troubles at Lisnave, for example, began to have direct repercussions on the workers employed there, as foreign governments and firms withdrew

C

their orders, among them a very large Swedish one. By June too, remittances from Portuguese migrants abroad had been slowed to a trickle, and unemployment had climbed to some 10 per cent. As the political situation degenerated into outright confrontation with the Communist party, the unions found themselves siding increasingly with the militants in order to make their strength felt in the near-anarchy. In the autumn, under the weak hand of Admiral Pinheiro de Azevedo's government, the Communists resorted to crippling strike action in the construction industry and other sectors; average wage settlements through the six-month period after March 1975 ran well ahead of the rate of inflation, at about 35 per cent. Portuguese goods were being steadily priced out of international markets, the country was living off imports financed by its savings, its gold and foreign exchange reserves. The reliance of the country's industrial growth under Caetano on low wages became increasingly apparent in the bankruptcies of firms unable to pay higher wages. It was left to democracy to pick up the pieces.

7   People power

The first clash between the parties that represented the people and the minority that controlled the government did not take long to materialise. On 1 May, just a year after the tumultuous May Day demonstrations with which Lisbon had celebrated its first days of freedom, a travesty of the same spectacle was held. The Communist union monopoly, Intersindical, held a small rally, attended by about 6000 people, in the First of May stadium in north-eastern Lisbon, to which neither the Socialists nor the Popular Democrats were officially invited. President Costa Gomes and prime minister Vasco Goncalves appeared on the platform beside the Communist leader, Alvaro Cunhal. Mario Soares angrily decided to lead a small band of his supporters to the rally, and managed to push his way past Communist stewards at the gate. But soldiers forcibly prevented him from getting on to the platform, and he had furious exchanges with near-by MFA leaders, who threatened to summon the leader of Portugal's largest party to appear before a military tribunal. He was escorted away by armed soldiers.

Next day, Soares was summoned to the president's palace, dressed down for the incident, and told to make up his quarrel with the Communists. But the Socialist leader was unrepentant that evening, and led a march of some 30,000 Socialists, shouting slogans as critical of the AFM as they dared. A Socialist statement said: 'It is time to say enough . . . The Socialist party will not allow a new dictatorship to be installed in this country.' The Popular Democrats came to the Socialists' support, saying, 'We consider what happened as treason to the people's vote and choice in the last election.' Both parties hinted that they were considering withdrawing their ministers from the government.

But Soares pulled back. Once again the president said he must meet the Communist leader, Alvaro Cunhal, and this time the Socialist leader agreed. In the early hours of 5 May, the two rivals put out an anodyne communiqué saying that they would 'defend the freedoms and advances made since the coup, mainly the measures taken for nationalisation and agrarian reform'. Costa Gomes hoped the agreement would lead eventually to the formation of a popular front government between the two parties. But only two days later Soares qualified his support for the agreement by insisting that the Communists should hold free union elections, and relinquish their hold on local government and the media. The flimsy truce lasted only a few days more, long enough for the two parties to agree to a military proposal extending nationalisation on 14 May.

But the MFA set the seal on its decision to ignore the election results on 6 May with a full-scale purge of the air force, hitherto the most conservative service branch. General Mendes Dias, its commander, was sacked and replaced by a younger man, General Jose Morais da Silva, who said he intended to create a 'revolutionary air force'. A deeply worried Soares concluded that confrontation with the MFA was now inevitable, and that persuasion had gone far enough.

The Socialist leader was presented with his *casus belli* three days later. One of Lisbon's last remaining non-Communist press voices was the newspaper *Republica*, run by Raul Rego, a veteran and often imprisoned opponent of the old right-wing dictatorship. In the by now classical pattern, Communists and left-wing militants persuaded printing workers to take over the paper, expel the old editorial staff, and turn it into yet another monotonously monolithic revolutionary broadsheet. But Rego was a highly committed Socialist, and a close personal friend of Mario Soares.

Expelled from his offices by the invading printers, Rego assembled an angry crowd of journalists and Socialists outside the building, and was joined by Mario Soares and Salgado Zenha, the minister of justice, for an all-night vigil. The ministry of information attempted to sidestep the problem by expelling the occupiers, and closing down the newspaper altogether. Soares replied furiously that the Socialist ministers would boycott cabinet meetings unless the paper was reopened under its original management, and called a demonstration of 50,000 people in central Lisbon on 22 May. The Socialist demonstrations were the first to be called in protest at a decision by the MFA, but Soares was too cautious to condemn the radical leaders in public.

Soares's defiance was enough, apparently, for Otelo. Exasperated by the political parties, he carried Rosa Coutinho's pre-election proposal a good deal further by suggesting that the parties be bypassed by soldier-worker committees which would act as the true representatives of the people. The MFA general assembly was convoked on 27 May to discuss Otelo's proposal and deal with the *Republica* dispute. But the old alliance which had defeated Rosa Coutinho's scheme came into operation once again. Communists united with moderate officers to oppose the move because Otelo's proposal was so clearly also aimed at the Communist party. Rosa Coutinho this time voted loyally with the Communist officers. Otelo's defeat took the crisis momentarily off the boil: the president and prime minister departed to attend the NATO summit in Brussels, and Soares again attended cabinet meetings to discuss the critical situation in Angola. The MFA, as a gesture on its part, gave a vague commitment to reopen the *Republica* offices.

There the matter stayed for two weeks. Then, on 16 June, the soldiers cleared out of the *Republica* offices and handed the paper back to the printers. In the evening, the printers had to be taken out under military protection through a hostile Socialist crowd, and the building was guarded until they returned in the morning. The issue took on wider dimensions two days later, when a large crowd of Communists and extreme left-wingers decided to march on the residence of the Archbishop of Lisbon. They were protesting against the Church's attempts to cut off electricity supplies to its own radio station, Radio Renascensa, which had been occupied by workers broadcasting anti-clerical propaganda for several months. A small crowd of Catholics tried to defend the building and were attacked for several hours by their opponents armed with sticks and iron bars, until troops came to rescue the Catholics. Soares immediately identified Radio Renascensa's cause with that of *Republica*, as part of the same general defence of press freedom, and he listed three conditions for staying in the cabinet: that media freedom be restored, and that elections be held to the central trades union body and to the local authorities.

The renewal of confrontation gave fresh impetus to Otelo's drive to do away with the parties. After consultations with Otelo, Vasco Goncalves decided to present the MFA general assembly with a compromise proposal to create Committees for the Defence of the Revolution, which would allow the civilian end of the worker-soldier committees to be controlled by the Communist party. Otelo refused to accept the new idea and, after eight hours' discussion, it was for the time being shelved. On 22 June a communiqué pledged the MFA to a pluralist road to Socialism, and repudiated 'the implantation of Socialism by violent or dictatorial means'.

For Soares, who welcomed the communiqué, it was a hollow victory: *Republica* was still run by the printers, none of his demands had been met, and his party had been saved from extinction only by the divisions of its opponents. The victory was also to be short-lived: on 9 July, the MFA assembly approved a compromise between Otelo's and the prime ministers' plans, which allowed for election to the workers' side of the councils by show of hands. In private they had both agreed to divide the councils between Goncalves's Communist supporters and Otelo's far-left supporters. The plan did not call for outright dissolution of the political parties, but for a parallel power structure alongside them.

Soares had reached the end of the road. On 11 July, he and Salgado

Zenha resigned from the government, and the same evening, at an emotional mass rally, Soares called for his followers to bring the country to a halt by demonstrations. The revolutionary process, he wrote to President Costa Gomes, 'is being led into a dead end with tragic consequences which can only favour counter-revolution'. Troops were put on alert in case of a coup attempt following the Socialist withdrawal. Privately, Soares made it clear that he would not consider joining another government led by Vasco Goncalves. Soares was to be criticised for making the main issue the removal of Vasco Goncalves as prime minister. But it was to be a highly effective tactic.

The PPD took about a week to withdraw from the government on 17 July. Less committed to Rego than Soares, they were also more ambivalent in the struggle with the MFA. Their leader, Sa Carneiro, had given up his post as secretary-general of the party in May owing to illness, and been replaced by Emidio Guerrero, a highly erratic, veteran anti-Salazarist crusader. Guerrero's appointment had been engineered by Marcello Rebelo da Sousa, on the basis that he would be more acceptable to MFA leaders, and that his age made him no more than a caretaker. With the domineering figure of Sa Carneiro gone, the party was otherwise in danger of descending into a gruelling personal contest for the succession between Pinto Balsemao and Magalhaes Mota. But Guerrero, although not a Communist, was considerably to the left of most of the party's leaders, not to mention its voters, and had to be restrained from some of his more extravagant speeches. He dithered for a while and finally decided that, on balance, the party should throw in its lot with the Socialists against the MFA. Growing militancy among the grassroots of the party was the major factor in Guerrero's decision.

On 16 July, thousands of Socialists marched through Lisbon shouting for the first time: 'The people are not with the MFA.' On 19 July 100,000 people responded to a call to rally in Lisbon by Soares, and defied Communist threats to stop them with road blocks. Communist vigilantes were armed, but when it became apparent that the Socialists would not give way, as Spinola had done ten months earlier, Goncalves agreed that COPCON troops should occupy the blocks and persuade the Communists to go home. With a few minor clashes, the rally passed off peacefully. For the first time, the Communists' and military bluff—that they alone were prepared to fight—had been called by the sheer weight of numbers of unarmed civilians. A similar demonstration of 50,000 people took place in Oporto.

For the first time, too, local organisers of the MDLP (see Chapter 11) took action into their own hands. Working through local branches of the CDS and PPD, and some local branches of the Socialist party, they had sufficient adherents to organise small meetings in the north, which they used as bases for marches on local Communist head-quarters, and for attacking the houses of known Communists. The MDLP action was extremely limited; it began with riots in Matosinha and Valenca on 19 July, which were followed by the sacking and burning of Communist offices the following day in Aveiro. The MDLP were only flexing their muscles, but got away with breaking the Communist stranglehold of fear operating on most northern towns, while giving the impression that the demonstrations were spontaneous.

The alliance between Goncalves's Communists and Otelo's extre-mists, which commanded a majority on both the Supreme Revolu-tionary Council and the MFA general assembly was, however, to last a while longer. In an effort to bring some sort of control to bear on a situation that seemed to be getting out of hand, the two groups decided to take the most blatantly dictatorial step yet. On 25 July they formed a triumvirate to run the country, consisting of Vasco Goncalves, Otelo de Carvalho and Costa Gomes. The president, ready to agree to anything that would provide a stopgap solution, was supposed to represent the moderate forces in the MFA: but non-Communist officers hardly found the president an advocate of their views. It was simultaneously announced that the government would be restructured.

8　The north raises the standard

The solution proved less than stopgap, because it rapidly became apparent that the new troika did not represent the views of fully a third of the Supreme Revolutionary Council, not to mention the mass of estranged army officers. Vasco and Otelo commanded no popular clout, and officers were beginning to wonder whether they commanded any military clout either. The moderate Socialist officers around Melo Antunes had been unimpressed by the indiscipline of the Portuguese armed forces, and by the radicals' failure to stop popular disturbances. Perhaps, after all, the extremists would crumble before popular discontent. Led by Melo Antunes, several members of the council temporarily boycotted its meetings.

Faced by open insubordination to the new rulers, Otelo, who returned from a pilgrimage to Fidel Castro's Cuba on 30 July, could only bluster at the airport, 'It is clearly becoming impossible to make a Socialist revolution by purely peaceful means.' In a reference to General Franco's massacre of Republican forces in the bullring at Badajoz at the beginning of the Spanish civil war, he said it might become necessary to put reactionaries into the Lisbon bullring. Yet Otelo was too able a man not to realise that the ground was being cut from under his feet: he was in danger of being too closely tied to Goncalves and the Communists, and finding the myth of his own popularity and leadership disappearing alongside theirs. Goncalves, who had confidently expected to form a government in the first week of August, found Otelo hesitating to support him. Hesitation became outright hostility when Goncalves offered Otelo the post of vice-premier, subordinated to himself.

At about the same time, the Catholic Church in the north began adding its weight to the three democratic parties, in open opposition to the MFA. The Church had lain low throughout the revolutionary process, for fear of itself becoming a victim. During the election campaign, church leaders instructed their followers only not to vote for atheist parties—a clear injunction not to vote Communist. The Portuguese episcopate had also fought to prevent Radio Renascensa being taken over, but still officially maintained its silence on Portuguese politics. Only the archbishop of Oporto, who had been considered dangerously left-wing under Salazar, felt he had secure enough public credentials to voice open criticism of the revolutionary process.

But with the country's political polarisation in the summer, individual bishops and priests took the initiative in denouncing the Communist bid for dictatorship from their pulpits. On 13 July, a crowd of some 10,000 catholics in Aveiro shouted political slogans to welcome Bishop Manuel Trinidade Coelho, president of the Portuguese episcopate, who had returned from a visit to Rome. As he walked from the station to Aveiro cathedral, the crowd shouted, '*Portugal, Portugal, no to communism.*' 'Freedom for the Church.' 'Freedom for Portugal.' 'Anarchy no, order yes.' The most militantly anti-Communist Church leader was the archbishop of Braga, Don Francisco Mario da Silva, who had been deliberately humiliated by pro-Communist customs officers on his way to an episcopal meeting in Brazil in June. The elderly archbishop was made to strip to be searched for smuggled currency. On 10 August, he got his own back in a fiery speech to 25,000 people outside the Cathedral. 'The Communists are hostile to God,' he declared, and the crowd marched on to the town's Communist headquarters, which they besieged until driven off after Communist gunfire had wounded twelve people.

The MDLP chose the beginning of August to unleash its first major wave of anti-Communist violence in the north. Communist head-quarters in Famalicao were sacked on 4 August, although not until two besiegers had been killed by shots fired from the Communist defenders inside. In the subsequent three weeks of rioting, about fifty Communist and MDP offices were sacked as the riots spread with a clockwork regularity across the north. On 7 August Otelo de Carvalho and General Fabiao went to Oporto to try to staunch the fighting and were humiliated by being booed and spat upon as they both left their cars. Marines were sent north to try to quell the rioting, to little effect.

On 8 August, Costa Gomes went through the motions of appointing Portugal's fifth government, and Goncalves's fourth, since April 1974. But the prime minister's death knell was sounded the same day. Melo Antunes and his moderate Socialist officers had had enough. They published a manifesto, which subsequently became known as the 'document of the nine' in which they openly proclaimed their alarm: the public myth of the indissoluble unity of the MFA was finally shattered. The signatories were headed by Antunes, Vitor Alves and Vitor Crespo. Four other members of the council of revolution signed—Major Costa Neves, Major Canto e Castro, Major Sousa e Castro and Major Vasco Lourenco. The list was rounded off by two men with formidable firepower at their disposal: Brigadier Pezarat Correia, commander of the southern military region, and Brigadier Franco Charais, commander of the central military region. The document declared roundly: 'The country finds itself deeply shaken,

deluded to a large extent of the great hopes it saw born with the MFA.'
The document called for a middle way between Russian-style
communism and Western European social democracy, but also for a
greater respect for public opinion. The new government, the nine
said, was 'lacking in credibility' and was 'manifestly incapable of
governing'.

Antunes was dropped from his post of foreign minister, and the
information minister, Correia Jesuino, gave warning that dire punishment would fall on the dissident officers. The triumvirate of Otelo,
Goncalves and Costa Gomes also condemned the document. In
retaliation, the nine boycotted the swearing in of the new cabinet, and
subsequent meetings of the Revolutionary Council. But as clashes
between large crowds and small groups of armed Communists trying
to defend their party headquarters spread across northern Portugal,
from Famalicao to Braganca to Braga to Oporto, the triumvirate was
in no position to clamp down on the officers without risking civil war.
Under the strain of the Antunes rebellion in the army and the civilian
rebellion in the north, the triumvirate fell apart.

The army chief of staff, General Fabiao, and the air force chief,
General Morais e Silva, allowed the nine's manifesto to circulate
through the army and air force. It gathered the support of some four-
fifths of serving officers in each, plainly exposing the MFA general
assembly for the unrepresentative body it was. Only in the navy, the
commander-in-chief, Admiral Pinheiro de Azevedo, a respected
professional soldier of almost no openly expressed political views,
refused to allow the document to be seen by officers. Pinheiro was a
solid figurehead, easily influenced by those about him. At the time he
accepted his role as a mouthpiece of the navy's leading radical officers,
led by Admiral Rosa Coutinho, without demur.

An attempt of sorts was made to discipline the nine for exposing the
divisions within the army to the public gaze. The Fifth Division had
demanded that 'exemplary punishment' should be inflicted on the
Antunes group on 9 August. All nine officers were formally suspended
from their posts, and a ban was imposed against officers—apart from
government ministers and the service chiefs—giving interviews to the
press. The ban was barely observed for a day, and protests from local
commanders restored both Pezarat Correia and Franco Charais to
their commands as southern and central military governors—which
were the only ones of any significance. Suspension from the Supreme
Revolutionary Council proved equally meaningless—the views of the
nine were to be as assiduously courted by the president as were those of
the radical rump on the council.

The army split was the first effective challenge to the left-wing
advance. By circulating his manifesto, Antunes had presented most

officers with the opportunity of registering opposition to Vasco Goncalves, without actually inciting them to overthrow him in a military coup. The extent of army support for Antunes's move in turn had its effect on the army and air force chiefs, Fabiao and Morais e Silva, always men to be led from behind, who had assented to circulating Antunes's document only because of the vague Socialist rhetoric in which it was couched. Antunes favoured a rapid and radical transformation of society, and still thought he was the best man to do it, by means of a pragmatic Socialism which recognised that people could not be carried along the revolutionary path too fast. Supported by Soares, whom Antunes thought represented the will of the people as expressed at the last election, supported by the outrage of the people in the north, he alone offered a middle course, he alone could save the revolution. Goncalves and Otelo were pushing Portugal too fast towards a Socialist society, and making violence inevitable.

But Antunes did not confuse his view with the democratic argument that the political authorities should be responsible to the people in elections. The last elections had strengthened his hand against the Communists, certainly, but he did not yet trust the Socialist intentions of civilian politicians, particularly Soares, nor did he consider that the Socialist vote gave Soares any greater claim than he to represent the true aspirations of the Portuguese people. Rather the reverse: the MFA had created the climate in which the Portuguese people had decided to vote Socialist; now the MFA must create the climate for a genuinely bloodless march towards Socialism. Antunes had travelled a long way, but he had yet to become a democrat. His argument, though, was good enough for men like Fabiao, who viewed the parties as divisive and unwelcome intrusions on the Portuguese scene, but who could see that something had to be done to assuage popular anger at the way the revolution was going.

Otelo proved rather slower in coming round to the view that the blood offering of Vasco Goncalves must be made to appease the wrath of the people. However intense the security chief's personal suspicions of the prime minister—which Goncalves had considerably stirred up by asking Otelo to become deputy prime minister—he viewed the Communists as a necessary ally; they were to be distrusted of course, but anything further right was to be even more distrusted. As always, he attempted the third course of publishing a document detailing his own, by now well-known, proposals for non-partisan 'neighbourhood councils' who would vote representatives to a national assembly. Many officers already suspected that Otelo would command few soldiers' allegiance in a showdown; but the Antunes group could not risk acting without his support. He had been in charge of the country's security command for too long not to have some army firepower behind him, and was known to have distributed considerable quantities of weapons to his supporters on the extreme left. Besides which, he might still command a residue of non-political loyalty among officers like Colonel Jaime Neves of the commandos.

The nine could not afford to wait for ever for Otelo's conversion. As Vitor Crespo put it on 14 August, an alternative must replace Goncalves so as to 'prevent any right-wing flag-wavers from gaining the support the left no longer enjoys'. The threat from the right was at last beginning to make itself felt. Reports were already reaching the regional commanders that MDLP members had infiltrated units in the central and northern military regions, as well as the organisation of anti-Communist groups in the north.

And, like Banquo's ghost, General Spinola made his presence felt from his resting place across the Atlantic in Rio de Janeiro. In an open letter to Costa Gomes, he told the man who had succeeded him as president:

> It is too late to make an appeal to you. The situation is clear. The present political direction of the country is irreconcilable with democracy ... I launch an appeal to the brave civilian combatants and to my brothers in arms that together all Portuguese within and outside the country may unite around the Democratic Movement for the Liberation of Portugal, which proposes the reconstruction of the country as a basis for the reconciliation of all Portuguese in liberty, dignity and justice.

For good measure, Spinola lambasted Melo Antunes as the author of a 'primitive Communist programme' in the months before the April 1974 coup. He could hardly have found a more tactless way of reminding the Portuguese that in July 1974 he had preferred the pro-Communist Vasco Goncalves as prime minister over Melo Antunes. But the genral's blast sent a chill through the group of nine. Pressures for a right-wing coup could build up inexorably if Vasco Goncalves stayed in power.

Antunes's task was made easier as the last vestiges of popular support for Goncalves and the Communists melted away. Alvaro Cunhal went north to make a speech at Alcobaca, only fifty miles from Lisbon, and barely escaped when the hall was besieged and pitched battles erupted between Communists and demonstrators outside. The Communist party secretary was led white-faced and trembling from the stadium, to cancel a rally scheduled five days later in Oporto. Where Cunhals's strong-arm men had denied the CDS the right to speak only five months ago, he himself was ironically prevented from furthering the cause which most of Portugal had come to abhor.

Northern troops for the first time opened fire that weekend on Communists at Ponte do Lima, where party members, defending their headquarters, had shot at the besieging crowd.

Goncalves made a forlorn attempt to rally support behind him on 18 August with a speech to 10,000 Communists in the Almada industrial district south of Lisbon, but the prime minister's speech was so raucous and demagogic that it only hardened opinion in the army against him. A general strike called for by the Communists on the following day proved so lamentable a failure that few party supporters dared observe it for fear of reprisals. Otelo the same day made up his mind to come out against Goncalves. Otelo's own extremist proposals for doing away with the parties received next to no support among officers, and to save face he had forborne to circulate them. President Costa Gomes delivered the government's death sentence when he said its life span could be 'expressed in days'. Goncalves's sole significant military ally, the commander of the northern military region, Brigadier Eurico Corvacho, was fired.

The charade still had a few days left to play itself out. Preliminary meetings between Otelo de Carvalho and Melo Antunes showed up significant differences between the two sides. On 21 August, Costa Gomes privately asked General Fabiao to form a government. The choice was adroit, because Fabiao's political confusion over the preceding months had made him acceptable to most parties, and partial to none; he was also, if anyone could be described as such, a respected figure in the army. And all along he had expressed the requisite doubts about the direction of the revolution. Fabiao accepted the task reluctantly. He was only too aware of the discontent mounting among his subordinate officers, and was loath to put himself in the firing line of leading a government should those officers one day turn against him.

Antunes insisted that Goncalves should be ousted by 25 August and, in a meeting with the president, Otelo took up the cry. But when the triumvirate met, neither the president nor the security chief could bring themselves to demand the third member's resignation, and so the task was handed down to the Supreme Revolutionary Council. As the group of nine had been suspended from the council, the left-wingers there were able to postpone the decision on whether Goncalves should stay by passing it on to the MFA general assembly, which was by now a far-left body containing revolutionary sergeants and privates. The assembly was given the task of restructuring the Revolutionary Council, which could only then debate Goncalves's future. In addition, the Revolutionary Council reinstated Brigadier Corvacho, Goncalves's chief ally in the army, to the post of northern military commander, from which he had been removed the week before. The prime minister took advantage of the council's delaying tactics to belatedly announce that he had been converted to Otelo's ideas for setting up 'peoples' power' committees to bypass the political parties. In this way he hoped to lure the maverick Otelo away from his support for the group of nine.

When Costa Gomes failed to fire Goncalves in time, the prime minister's opponents continued to hang back from staging a coup to depose him. Both Otelo and Antunes still hoped the issue could be resolved peacefully. But their first choice of prime minister, General Carlos Fabiao, concluded that hesitation was a sign of weakness, and on 25 August declared he would under no circumstances become prime minister. In anger, the president issued a statement saying that Goncalves would remain head of government. But Costa Gomes had begun to fall back on the idea of taking over the functions of prime minister himself, or of asking a political unknown, the commander of the Portuguese navy, Admiral Pinheiro de Azevedo, to do the job.

The president was lapsing into a state of almost total indecision. He was veering sharply between a sense of loyalty towards Goncalves and a recognition that civil war might break out unless Gocalves went. On 27 August, Costa Gomes appeared at a remarkable rally outside the presidential palace at Belem to address a large far-left crowd that had marched from central Lisbon. The crowd cheered a rabid speech by Vasco Goncalves, and booed the president's lukewarm references to the need for a degree of political pluralism. Immediately after this apparent display of support for Goncalves, Melo Antunes delivered his ultimatum: unless the prime minister was dismissed forthwith, he and other moderate officers were prepared to travel north, call on loyalist troops and anti-Communist civilians to follow them, and start a civil war if necessary. The commander of the central military region, Franco Charais, announced that he would rally his troops behind Antunes.

Costa Gomes hesitated no longer. On 29 August, he dismissed Goncalves. Admiral Pinheiro de Azevedo was the new prime minister. But even now, the president could not go the whole way: the former prime minister was to be given the consolation prize of commander in chief of the armed forces, a post previously held by Costa Gomes in his capacity as president. The news was greeted with incredulity among the moderates in the armed forces and in the political parties. 'It would be absurd', said Mario Soares, 'to retain the man responsible for the divisions inside the armed forces and place him in a much more important position than the one he now holds.' The group of nine flatly rejected the appointment, and once again played on the spectre of a general uprising of the armed forces, in anticipation of which all forces were placed on alert on 30 August.

A succession of prominent military commanders paraded their

objections to the new commander, including the governors of Madeira and the Azores, the chief of staff of Portuguese forces in Angola, and the formerly left-wing air force chief, General Morais e Silva. On 3 September, the air force and army chiefs refused to attend a general meeting of the MFA assembly and held their own service assemblies, which called for Goncalves to step down from his new post. Only the navy turned up to the general assembly, and, under Admiral Rosa Coutinho, who was substituting for Admiral Pinheiro de Azevedo, voted for Goncalves to stay. In the face of such near-unanimity, Goncalves at last two days later resigned from public office.

The first storm had blown over. But worse was to come. The triumphant group of nine was reinstated to the Supreme Revolutionary Council, tipping the balance there in favour of the anti-Communist forces, although Otelo de Carvalho's supporters remained an unpredictable quantity. Portugal's unknown new prime minister busied himself with forming a government—not an easy task, as the rival Socialist and Popular Democratic Parties began to argue about the number of ministers the Communists should have in the new cabinet. Vasco Goncalves, the loyal and defeated military ally of Alvaro Cunhal's Communists, retired to daily life in a working-class district near Lisbon.

9   All eyes on Portugal

From the day of the coup in April 1974 until the dénouement of the revolution in November 1975, Portugal was never long out of international consciousness. It excited a wider world press over those nineteen months than any other running European story. It aroused first a welcome from America and Western Europe, that under such a safe conservative figure as Spinola Portugal had thrown off the mantle of dictatorship, then apprehension about the direction events were taking after Spinola was overthrown. And it attracted hordes of commentators, Intelligence officers, interested political observers and young revolutionaries to observe at first-hand Europe's first real revolution since the war.

The American secretary of state, Henry Kissinger, decided to play the crisis in Portugal in low key. For more than a year now, the American Central Intelligence Agency had been savaged for its role in 'destabilising' Chile in the early 1970s, in helping along the military coup that overthrew the country's Marxist President Allende, in financing his opponents, and in discouraging foreign money from saving his bankrupt regime. Kissinger could not afford a repeat of the American performance in Portugal. None the less, he had deep private misgivings about what was happening there, and at his most pessimistic saw Portugal as the first of a series of West European dominoes, governments containing Communist ministers, who would chip away at the NATO alliance, and would sap the American public's will to keep American forces in Europe. Portugal's coup was followed by a conflict between Greece and Turkey over Cyprus which weakened NATO's position on its south-eastern flank. Political crises, partly induced by the world-wide recession, would also, he feared, weaken NATO in Portugal, Italy and France, and would keep post-Franco Spain out of NATO.

Because of the weakness of his domestic position, Kissinger confined himself to financial support for the anti-Communist forces in Portugal, to counter the considerable Russian support—estimated at $10 million a month being channelled through the Moscow Nardodny bank in London—to the Portuguese Communist party. The secretary of state soon decided to replace the career diplomat Stuart Scott, who was Washington's ambassador in Lisbon from before the coup. Scott had assured Kissinger that rumours of a Communist takeover were exaggerated, but by early 1975 the country's forced march to the left seemed to disprove him. Scott's successor was Frank Carlucci, a diplomat with considerable experience in world trouble-spots, and one whom left-wing political forces immediately attacked as a living example of American interventionism. But Carlucci scarcely put a foot wrong. Never underestimating the danger of a revolutionary seizure of power, he advised Kissinger to place his hopes on the growing rift between the Socialist and Communist parties. The Americans maintained close contacts with non-Communist forces in the army, such as General Galvao de Melo, in spring 1975, and the group of nine in the summer, but Mario Soares's steadfastness in the face of the threat from the Communists came to be the main repository of their hopes.

Much of the credit for persuading the Americans to back the Socialists against the Communists, and so avoid the brickbats of the European left, who could scarcely charge that America was acting as the agent of reaction, lay with the West German Social Democratic party. The West German chancellor, Helmut Schmidt, and the party chairman, Willy Brandt, were close friends of Mario Soares, and had long expounded the view that social democracy in Europe was a better bulwark against Communism than the right. The Social Democrats provided money for the Portuguese Socialists, and when it began to look as if the only party that would be allowed to compete with the Communists on their own ground in the 1975 elections was the Socialist one, Schmidt had no trouble in securing American support for Soares. Kissinger often wondered about Soares's strength of resolution, but his pro-Western attitudes and his democratic beliefs left no room for doubt.

Political parties in other European countries did a little towards trying to help the alternatives to the Socialists—the British Conservatives, for example, on the urgings of a bright young research officer, Michael Young, offered campaigning and television training for the Centre Democrats. The party also managed to build up links with the Giscardiens in France, and with inter-European conservative groups under the aegis of a Swedish conservative, Carl Bildt. The Popular Democrats quixotically sought recognition from European Social Democratic parties, failed to get it, and refused to be connected with any European groups futher to the right. But neither of them could compete with the Socialist party's appeal for the West Germans and the Americans.

Part of Kissinger's low-profile policy in Portugal consisted in dampening international monetary fears, as Portugal's economy sped out of control. In December 1975 the Americans offered $20 million in economic aid, as a token gesture of confidence in Portugal's future, and to repudiate in advance any suggestion that the Americans were encouraging a flight of capital. The Common Market countries proved much more cautious, and were only prodded into an offer of $90 million towards the end of 1975, after the turn of the political tide. But Christopher Soames, the EEC's commissioner for external affairs, offered encouraging noises in early 1975 about the prospect of a democratic Portugal's entering the Community.

The EEC option was central to the Western democracies' whole approach to Portugal at the time. Portugal was caught between two vices, that of Africa and that of Europe, a dilemma symbolised by the power struggle within Portugal itself. The coup had come as a rebellion by army officers against Portugal's colonial adventures. But to a man— and that included Melo Antunes—the left-wing soldiers saw Portugal's future as part of the non-aligned third world, linked to Africa, led by a progressive, authoritarian government. The younger, European-orientated middle class that had grown up in the late 1960s didn't see it like that at all; nor did Portugal's people. The three democratic parties—Soares's Socialists, Sa Carneiro's Popular Democrats, Freitas do Amaral's Centre Democrats—were from the first blindly committed to becoming 'European', which they equated with abandoning Portugal's old membership of the European Free Trade Area and joining the EEC.

Their choice had little to do with economics: Portugal's inefficient farming methods meant that in only two products—tomato paste and wine—could it undersell the EEC, and in only one industrial sector— textiles—was Portugal competitive. EEC membership, without a long transitional period, would expose Portugal quickly to the bracing winds of international competition. On economic grounds, some EEC members were equally unenthusiastic: they would have to contribute more to the social and regional funds to help their impoverished southern neighbour. But for once their political will extended to trying to encourage the democratic, pro-European parties in Portugal, and the parties were glad of all the help from the democratic parties that they could get. When Portugal's weak president Costa Gomes attended the NATO summit in Brussels in May, he was mercilessly chivvied by the Europeans present, socialists and conservatives alike, about the direction of events in Portugal.

West European countries were firm but calm in their attitudes towards a government containing Communists also being a member of NATO. In early 1975, the NATO countries hinted that Portugal would not be welcome as a member of the alliance's nuclear planning group, which had access to highly classified NATO material, and the Portuguese gracefully bowed out. But the country's actual membership of the alliance was never called into question.

In the event of an outright victory by the far left in Portugal, the Americans had only one contingency plan prepared. Portugal's membership of the alliance was important above all because of the country's strategically vital possession of the Azores islands in the Atlantic. The Americans had an air base at Lajes in the Azores and an underwater terminal to monitor Russian submarine movements in the Atlantic. The Americans had also used the islands as a refuelling station for planes carrying supplies to Israel during the 1973 Middle East war, when the rest of oil-conscious Europe refused to help.

About 1 million Azoreans lived in the United States compared to a population of only about 300,000 on the islands themselves, and many Azoreans had closer family ties with the United States than with Portugal. The islands were dominated by a handful of large, conservative landowners, and a relatively contented rural population. When the local Communist party attempted to flex its muscles in the islands, a backlash quickly developed. The military governor of the Azores, General Altino Pinto de Magalhaes, was a determined anti-Communist, who insisted that he would resist Lisbon attempts to inflict Socialist policies upon the islanders. A separatist group was born in the spring of 1975, the Front for the Liberation of the Azores, FLA (which had a sister organisation, the Front for the Liberation of Madeira in Portugal's other Atlantic island), with its own paper, *O Milhafre*, and editor, Jose de Almeida, who ran it in the summer of 1975 from the United States. Discussions took place in July 1975 between American officials and FLA members on the viability of an independent Azores if Portugal's far-left government continued in office.

The same month, anti-Communist crowds sacked the party's head-quarters throughout the islands, and drove members into virtual hiding. An anxious Supreme Revolutionary Council in Lisbon temporarily shelved plans to set up a left-wing administrative council to govern the islands. By the end of August, they were forced to give the islands nearly full autonomy to stave off independence demands, and General Pinto was declaring that his loyalty to the government in Lisbon took second place to his loyalty to the Portuguese people. In the event, the swing to the right in Portugal made any formal independence bid by the Azores unnecessary, and the Americans were able to shelve their plans, although FLA activity sputtered on.

United States caution was such that only at the height of the struggle against the far left in the summer did the Americans issue a direct challenge against Russian interference in Portugal. It happened shortly after an attack in *Pravda* on 8 August, criticising Western Europe for interference in Portugal: 'Is it not time,' *Pravda* asked blithely, 'to begin fulfilling the obligations undertaken by the representatives of the western powers concerning non-interference in the internal affairs of other people?' On 14 August Kissinger hit back with a blunt warning. Russia, he said,

should not assume it has the option, either directly or indirectly, to influence events contrary to the right of the Portuguese people to determine their own future. The involvement of external pressures for this purpose in a country which is an old friend and ally of ours is inconsistent with any principle of European security.

Kissinger set out his own sympathies:

The attempt by an anti-democratic and doctrinaire minority to thwart this desire [for democracy in Portugal] is meeting irresistible and growing popular resistance. We sympathise with those moderate elements who seek to build Portugal by democratic means. We will oppose and speak out against the efforts of a minority that appears to be subverting the revolution to its own purposes. The Portuguese people should know that we and all the democratic countries of the west are deeply concerned about their future and stand ready to help a democratic Portugal.

The blunt message was that America viewed Portugal as a test of the Russians' faith in signing the Helsinki declaration on European security earlier in the year. The warning was probably instrumental in getting the Russians to tell Cunhal that his struggle should stop short of provoking civil war. Subsequent reports suggest that a power struggle was going on at the time in the Kremlin between those like the KGB chief, Alexander Shelepin, who believed that the Portuguese struggle should be intensified and internationalised, and who were encouraging an uninterrupted flow of arms and revolutionaries from Cuba, Chile, Czechoslovakia and other countries to Portugal, and those like Brezhnev who did not want events to get out of hand. By insisting that America would not accept a Russian-aided Communist takeover of Portugal lying down, Kissinger may have swung the argument Brezhnev's way.

Brezhnev was probably equally concerned to prevent the black image of Portugal's Communists rubbing off on the other Communist parties of Western Europe who were proclaiming democratic ideals. In 1975, the Russian leader appeared to be encouraging the so-called 'Eurocommunist' parties, considering their democratic ideals to be temporary and tactical. By weakening NATO, the Russians hoped that strong Western Communist parties would be profoundly beneficial to the Warsaw pact in Eastern Europe. The fight between the Portuguese Socialists and Communists came as a profound embarrassment to the two major Eurocommunist parties in Italy and in France. The Portuguese Communists' baldly anti-democratic statements in March were seized upon by Christian Democratic leaders in Italy as an occasion to stage a walkout from observing the Italian Communist party's congress the same month, and so to set Italian voters wondering about the democratic claims of their own Communists.

Over the summer months, the Italian Communists went out of their way to disassociate themselves from their Portuguese comrades, and drew some Russian criticism for doing so. On 16 August, the Italian Communists secured the signature of Italy's small Socialist party to a document to obscure the issues in Portugal by calling for an alliance between 'the democratic parties, in particular the Communists and Socialists, and between them and the armed forces movement'. Mario Soares, then engaged in a fight to the death with the Communists and MFA radicals, cannot have appreciated the call from his Italian sister party. But to some extent he had deserved the slight: when addressing a Socialist campaign rally on a solidarity trip to Rome to help the Italian Socialists in the local election campaign in June, he said he wished that Portugal had as reasonable a Communist party as Italy had. His Italian Socialist colleague, who had been stressing the anti-democratic dangers of voting Communist in Italy, looked uncomfortable; as, indeed, he had reason to be when the votes were counted, and his party won less than a quarter of the votes won by the Communists.

The Communist-Socialist conflict in Portugal caused a mini-conflict within the coalition of the left between the Communists and the Socialists in France. Despite a claim to have joined the Italians in pursuing democratic methods, the French Communist leader, Georges Marchais, came out in April with expressions of solidarity for his Portuguese comrades. The French Socialists had to disagree, and after the Communist newspaper *L'Humanité* had denounced Socialist demonstrations in Lisbon in July as 'fascist', a meeting was arranged in August to try to patch the quarrel up. But the French Socialist leader, François Mitterand, refused to attend the meeting, and instead sent a message asking the Communists to be more self-critical; nothing came of the meeting. The dispute eventually passed under the bridge, but it still left doubts in many French minds as to the true extent of Marchais's conversion to democracy.

10 Anarchy

The civil war of which Mario Soares had so often warned was never nearer to breaking out than in the next three months. The forces of the extreme left had taken a battering, but had not been beaten in open conflict. The sacrificial offering of Vasco Goncalves was seen by many as a strategic move by Otelo and the Communists, not as a major defeat. The forces resisting them—the Socialists, the northern farmers, the majority of non-political officers, the MDLP co-ordinators—were still testing their strength, unsure how far they could go without provoking the bloodshed all had striven for so long to avoid. But civil wars are made by people willing to die for their beliefs. In Portugal, beliefs were passionately held, but not to the point of self-sacrifice. The heavy element of bluff that had allowed the extreme left to railroad the Portuguese people during the first phase of the revolution had been exposed. But no one could be sure that the democratic forces were not themselves bluffing. And the game of bluff and counter-bluff, each side trying to make the other believe it was the stronger, more committed, more prepared to fight for its beliefs, led Portugal to the brink of a bloodless and verbose anarchy.

The man who presided over the chaos was, on the face of it, an unlikely choice. Admiral Joao Batista Pinheiro de Azevedo was one of a rare breed that history plucks from obscurity to play a temporary but important role, and then forgets. No one had ever seen a potential statesman in the admiral. He just happened to be in the right place at the right time, and he exceeded the little that was expected of him. He was a vital connecting link in the chain. Without him, the passage from a far-left dictatorship to a moderate democracy might have been a slower, more traumatic one.

Pinheiro was chosen because he offended no one. Such political opinions as he had offered in the past seemed to favour the left-wing revolutionaries. His political views under the pre-1974 dictatorship had followed the right-wing orthodoxy of the time. For the most part he voiced no view at all. Like most military men who reach the top of their profession, he was a prudent opportunist. But military opportunists, unlike civilian ones, are at the last moment called upon to make decisions. Where a political opportunist can play for time, weave and negotiate to find a compromise solution, an easy way out, soldiers at some stage in their careers have to issue orders which may result in the deaths of the men they command. The admiral, on his way up the hierarchy, had skilfully moulded his opinions to those of his superiors. But now he was the commander, alone in the field, no longer dependent on orders from above. Like the good soldier he was, pragmatic, not over-intelligent, starting with not very strong ideological preconceptions, he faced up to his responsibility. Portugal's far left politicians hoped he was in their pocket—especially since his *chef du cabinet* was Commander Ramiro Correia of the now defunct Fifth Division. Portugal's democrats looked with dismay on the admiral's past reputation. But Admiral Pinheiro de Azevedo showed that he could take a decision on its own merits.

Pinheiro's cabinet was formed only after three weeks of wrangling, as the Communists fought for equal representation with the Popular Democrats. It was hardly an auspicious start. The cabinet was largely patched together by Melo Antunes, who returned to it as foreign minister. The number of military men fell to five, and the Communists were left with only one cabinet post—Alvaro Veiga de Oliveira as minister of public works. There were four Socialists and two Popular Democrats, a party line-up which squared with the outcome of the April election. The Socialists were evenly divided between their left-wing (Lopes Cardoso) and right-wing (Salgado Zenha) as minister of finance. Party leaders stayed out of the government, and the Communist leader, Alvaro Cunhal, boycotted the swearing-in ceremony on 19 September.

Cabinets, of course, had had little power in Portugal since the revolution. Melo Antunes clearly intended to dominate the government from his post on the Supreme Revolutionary Council. And from the start Mario Soares showed he could dance to the tune of Antunes's peculiar brand of radical Socialism. As the Socialist leader said in an interview to *The Times* on 22 September: 'Our programme is not a programme to correct the most unjust aspects of capitalism, but to destroy capitalism.' Soares had always felt the need to appease as far as possible the prevailing army faction, and Antunes was closely sympathetic to his own party. But the government drew an additional degree of authority from its claim to be more representative of the Portuguese people than previous governments. The subtle Antunes, as an archetypal *éminence grise*, was a strangely complementary figure to the bluff, homespun, short-tempered but warm-hearted prime minister.

The size of Pinheiro's task came home to him with a bang just thirty-six hours after he was sworn in as prime minister. A bomb exploded outside the prime minister's summer flat in a naval building on the waterfront at Cascais. The prime minister was shaken but unharmed. No one discovered who was responsible, as always. It was a symbol of the administrative collapse that was to follow.

The forces of the right and the moderate left had united to overthrow Vasco Goncalves, while the precarious unity of the extreme left had fallen apart. In the ensuing weeks of stalemate between the two main camps, the fissiparous forces in each camp came to the surface. Portugal came to face the danger of a death of a thousand cuts, as rival interest groups tried to assert themselves in the uncertain vacuum of authority under the sixth provisional government. The worst fragmentation took place in the army: Otelo, caught off balance by the drive to force Goncalves out of office, was now determined to make a show of force. Supporters of Otelo had taken advantage of the inter-regnum after Goncalves's resignation to form a popular power group of soldiers and non-commissioned officers called Soldados Unidos Venceremos (SUV)—Soldiers United Will Win—to back up the demands of the dwindling group of radical officers around Otelo. SUV, although, a factional body, and therefore operating in flagrant viola-tion of the Portuguese military code, was given free rein—because many of its members came from the military police, which was among the most radical units of the Portuguese army.

SUV's first concern was to disrupt military discipline. As Angola's three rival liberation movements moved closer to full-scale civil war, Portuguese attempts to organise the evacuation of the growing stream of Portuguese settlers fleeing the impending conflict were being endangered. Portugal's existing garrison in Angola had become increasingly inadequate to the task of keeping peace in Luanda and its hinterland, to which most of the refugees had converged, and where the bitterest struggle for power between the liberation movements was in progress. In late September 2000 soldiers, many of them from the military police units, were ordered out to Luanda to reinforce the Portuguese garrison. Reluctant to fight, and suspecting that the government was trying to disperse abroad the more radical regiments, the military police sat tight in their barracks and refused to go. Twelve military police officers who opposed the mutiny were 'dismissed' by their brother officers. On 25 September, some 2000 SUV soldiers marched through Lisbon calling for 'reactionaries' to get out of their barracks.

SUV was the biggest, but not the only group to split away from the unified command of the armed forces. The Revolutionary Action Group of Army Privates, founded at about the same time, emerged as a trades union for its members, fighting 'the structure and discipline of the bourgeois army', its aim the betterment of conditions and pay in the lower ranks. Another group of crippled war veterans actually succeeded in taking over the offices of Lisbon's main radio station on 25 September and broadcast demands for proper compensation and rehabilitation into civilian life. A demonstration of war veterans outside Sao Bento palace on 28 September was only dispersed by gunfire.

Most of the interest groups were acting quite independently of one another, although SUV leaders consulted frequently with Otelo. But the protest threatened to spill over into violence when the radical soldiers ran up against another pressure group—the penniless, dispossessed refugees from Angola, who bitterly resented Portugal's revolution and the way it had been responsible for depriving them of their homes and livelihoods. On 24 September, for example, military police had to fire in the air in Rossio square in central Lisbon to disperse a crowd of refugees who had assembled for a demonstration.

Perhaps most ominous was the flow of weapons into the hands of the far left. Military sources estimated at 20,000 the number of guns that had disappeared from arsenals in army barracks, and an officer admitted distributing 1000 weapons to left-wing civilians groups. The officer in question, Captain Fernandes, was a close friend of Otelo, and had helped to draft Otelo's manifesto for a 'people's power' government. Otelo, mildly annoyed by the theft, called it 'inopportune', but added, 'as the guns are in leftish hands, for me they are in good hands'. The worst outbreak of violence took place on 27 September, when a mob of demonstrators sacked and burnt the Spanish embassy in Lisbon to protest against the execution on that day of five terrorists by General Franco. Troops, some of them SUV members, who were sent to protect the embassy stood by passively. Some of the soldiers joined in the burning and looting of the embassy.

Pinheiro had had enough. A stand had to be made by the government, however slender the resources at its disposal. On 29 September, he went on television to state unequivocally: 'the disorders of the last few days have surpassed all the limits of tolerance and have placed at risk the continuation not only of effective authority, but of any authority and even our national independence'. He announced that a new internal security force would be created, the Military Intervention Force, under the command of an obscure professional officer, Brigadier-General Nunes Egidio, to bypass Otelo's uncontrollable military empire. Those long-standing bones of contention, Radio Clube Portuguesa and Radio Renascensa, were to be taken over. The Portuguese armed forces were placed on a state of general alert.

All this was easier said than done. Two squads of COPCON soldiers were finally ordered into the radio stations the following day to muzzle the stream of anti-government propaganda that had flowed out of them during the preceding weeks. The parachute unit ordered into Radio Clube Portuguesa simply settled into the studio's easy chairs, and watched the broadcasters get on with it. The force occupying Radio

Renascensa divided into two groups, some favouring stopping the broadcasts, some against. Otelo's action in agreeing to send in the troops was not popular among his military followers, and in the evening he was besieged at the ministry of information by a left-wing crowd, which he addressed from a balcony. The versatile general tried to pacify the jeers of the crowd by claiming he was only obeying orders; and at length he agreed to lead a march on the presidential palace at Belem.

Pinheiro was made of sterner stuff. The following day, 26 September, he called in one of the few effective regiments left, the Amadora commandos under Colonel Jaime Neves. Before dawn, the commandos cut off Radio Renascensa's transmitters. Neves's men also moved on the offices of the newspaper *Republica*, but were blocked by left-wingers from the light artillery regiment, RAL-1. The Radio Clube Portuguesa, to forestall a possible commando takeover, started broadcasting relatively non-controversial material. Pinheiro, appeased by the gesture, ordered his rebellious soldiers out of the building, and allowed Radio Clube to stay on the air. But the left-wing soldiers in the studios, to demonstrate their solidarity with the broadcasters, stayed until persuaded to move out in the afternoon by Otelo himself.

The civilian leaders could only stand and watch as the struggle fizzled on between the army factions. On the day that Neves's commandos were called in, the Socialists and Popular Democrats organised another rally to back the prime minister. That evening the Socialists extravagantly claimed that their rally had forestalled a coup by the extreme left: the prime minister, they said, was to have been seized, and newspapers and radio stations were to have been taken over. The party was probably only trying to give itself a role under circumstances in which it was powerless to act. The coup plot was the first in a series of charges and counter-charges giving warning of imminent insurrections which flew about between both sides, none of which ever materialised. The truth was that in Portugal every faction was groping around in a fog, each accusing the others of trying to steal an unfair advantage, each side just hoping to be in the right place to seize power when the fog cleared.

The indecisive confrontation over the radio stations was only a fore-taste of what was to come. Left-wing units increasingly refused to obey orders aimed at diminishing their influence. On 3 October, seventy soldiers stationed near the southern Communist stronghold of Beja refused an order transferring them to the Azores. A loyalist parachute unit from Tancos failed to budge them from their barracks. In Lisbon, the left-wing RAL-1 commander, Major Dinis de Almeida, rejected an order to redistribute arms from his rebellious garrison to the garrisons of pro-government forces. But the worst flare-up took place in Oporto.

On 4 October, General Pires Veloso, the new northern military commander, ordered his troops to break up a sit-in by thirty soldiers from a military driving school whose unit had been disbanded for refusing to obey orders. An auxiliary artillery regiment of 700 men, loyal to the dismissed pro-Communist northern military commander, Brigadier Eurico Corvacho, began its own sit-in in protest at the Serra do Pilo barracks.

On 8 October, Oporto's Popular Democrats held a march of solidarity with Pinheiro through the city, and some of the crowd broke away towards the barracks. Who started the shooting at the barracks is still unclear. But the eighty wounded in the fighting over the next hour came exclusively from among the Popular Democrats; pistol-toting soldiers inside the barracks were unharmed. The shooting only broke off when soldiers and police in armoured cars arrived to send the Popular Democrats home. Pires Veloso angrily threatened to bomb the barracks after the clash, but later toned down his remarks.

The rebellion by the artillerymen in Oporto was the most serious setback yet to the government's chances of winning a semblance of control. Not for the first time, Portugal's army leadership was split over what to do about the mutineers. Pires Veloso, a tough, practical soldier, was for starving the rebels out if necessary. Pinheiro and Melo Antunes agreed that surrender to the mutineers' demands would be dangerous, and were backed up by the democratic parties. But President Costa Gomes and the army chief of staff, General Fabiao, were for conciliation.

Fabiao, with whom the final decision on affairs of military discipline lay, proposed to make a trip up to Oporto and then reach a decision. On the morning of 14 October, he arrived quietly at the barracks for three hours of talks with the rebel leaders. He came out to announce that the left-wingers' main demand—for the reinstatement of the driving school unit—would be met. The sit-in was over. Pinheiro and Pires Veloso were incensed. In an effort to limit the damage caused by Fabiao's display of weakness, Veloso fired the commanders of the left-wing soldiers, an action which drew renewed protests from the artillery-men. Fabiao was not to know that his weakness that day would cost him his job a little more than a month later.

Fabiao's surrender gave new heart to the left-wing groups, and on 22 October left-wingers and soldiers moved into Radio Renascensa, took over the by now unguarded transmitter, and started broad-casting again. The following day, the emboldened Communists came out for their biggest demonstration since the anti-Communist violence of the summer. The government, bemused by the speed of events, did nothing. In retaliation, on 23 October, right-wingers from the Portuguese Liberation Army set off bombs under the cars of left-wing officers, including Commander Ramiro Correia. No one, as usual, was injured. But the bombs prodded Otelo into action. He put his COPCON forces on alert, without consulting Pinheiro. The prime minister appealed for calm once again. 'A climate of general unrest exists,' he told the nation in a television broadcast, 'which is favourable to the right. The situation is critical because of the extreme left's and the Communist party's adventurous policies.' On 25 October, Pinheiro flew north to troubled Oporto to rally the forces of moderation, and spoke to a large demonstration of about 100,000 people organised by the three democratic parties.

Power had become diffused among so many groups in Portugal that no side could be certain of its relative strength. Pinheiro's strength had come to rest on the support of the democratic civilian parties, and on Melo Antunes's careful chaperoning of the Supreme Revolutionary Council. But the lower ranks of the army were disintegrating under ideological pressure, and in the higher commands were two men whom Pinheiro could not trust: Otelo, whose revolutionary conscience was growing by the minute; and Fabiao, who was determined not to be the man blamed by posterity for leading his country away from revolution. So Pinheiro and Antunes could do only one thing: sidestep the natural chains of command and try to unite what disciplined and loyal troops remained. As it happened, the man to perform such a task was ready and waiting at Pinheiro's shoulder; he was an unknown young soldier, Lieutenant-Colonel Ramalho Eanes, whose rise to power will be charted in the next chapter.

Many of the moderate left-wing soldiers were suspicious of Antunes's attempt to create a disciplined force. On 31 October, Brigadier Franco Charais, commander of the central military region, voiced his fear that the left was playing into the hands of a right-wing coup. The Communist leader, Alvaro Cunhal, himself professed alarm at the way things were going. The biggest danger, he said, would come on 11 November, the day of Angola's independence. For the refugees, the only hope of a return to their home and possessions in Angola lay in a victory by the non-Marxist forces there. An agreement was reported to have been reached between one of the leaders of ex-President Spinola's exile organisation, the Democratic Movement for the Liberation of Portugal (MDLP), Colonel Santos e Castro, and Holden Roberto's National Front for the Liberation of Angola. The right-wing Angolan nationalist leader agreed that the Portuguese refugees should go back if he won the war. The MDLP was concerned at the time, first, to prevent Portugal recognising the Marxist Popular Movement for the Liberation of Angola as the new government of the country and, second, to try to bring the remaining soldiers in Angola on Roberto's side.

Cunhal was right about the refugees' real objectives. But he over-estimated their influence within the MDLP, which was itself declining in strength. Spinola and his chief political adviser, Manuel Cotta Dias, both agreed that a return to colonial involvement would be dangerous for Portugal, not because they would not have preferred a slower colonial pull-out than was in fact taking place, but because they felt that all available resources had to be concentrated on the domestic scene. Pinheiro and Antunes went all the way they could towards accommodating refugee demands, and on 9 November announced they would leave Luanda without conferring the seal of Portuguese approval on any one of the liberation movements. MDLP leaders were satisfied, and promptly communicated to their friends in Lisbon that a coup attempt to forestall Angolan independence was out of the question. They needed more time to organise, they claimed, and wanted the left to make the first move. The MDLP failed to mention it was also too weak.

The danger of a coup attempt from the left was always the more considerable. The left-wing groups felt that time was running out for them, as their unpopularity in the country grew; and that a show of force while the right was still scattered had to come soon. They argued that, as in the Russian revolution of October 1917, a small and deter-mined group of militants with enough weapons and sympathisers in the armed forces stood as good a chance of taking advantage of the prevailing chaos to seize power as they were ever likely to get. Since the summer, a growing number of left-wingers from other countries had converged on Lisbon from Spain, Chile, Cuba and Uruguay, and even Czechoslovakia. This foreign army was said to number 9000 men, although the figure was probably exaggerated.

The main problem for the left was its own lack of unity. Many of the left-wingers belonged to diverse revolutionary groups and lacked common goals. Most of them saw in Otelo their potential leader, but Otelo hesitated for several weeks to join them in an all-out attack on the government. The Communist party, which previously had the strongest and most militant backing on the left, thoroughly distrusted Otelo, and the feeling was reciprocated. The Communists themselves were being torn by an internal conflict. Western warnings to the Soviet Union that the behaviour of the Portuguese Communist party was being taken as a test of Russian sincerity under the 1975 treaty of Helsinki, which pledged the signatories to non-interference in the internal affairs of other countries, had had some effect. There is little doubt that the official, but by no means the unqualified, Soviet message to Alvaro Cunhal was to play it cool during September and November. Cunhal's own position appeared to be under threat from the orthodox, pro-Brezhnev members of his party, in particular the deputy leader, Octavio Pato, and from Aboim Ingles, a prominent Portuguese exile who had only returned from Moscow in September.

The Communist leadership was divided over whether to throw in its lot with the far left in a probably suicidal bid for power, or to adopt a longer-term strategy of caution. Cunhal feared his party would be banned if the right regained control after a bungled coup attempt by the left. But if he steered clear of Otelo's adventurers, he hoped the party would survive to fight another battle. The triumphal local election victory of the Italian Communists in June 1975 had shown that after all there was something to be gained from trying to win popular support and adopting non-revolutionary tactics.

Coup fever reached a peak in the fortnight leading up to 11 November. Just twelve days earlier, on 31 October, Alvaro Cunhal warned that 'men from the 28 September and 11 March coups are preparing another coup on Portugal'. Left-wingers charged that army manoeuvres arranged north of Lisbon during the week preceding Angolan independence day would end in a coup. On 3 November, Mario Soares gave warning of a coup threat from the far left. Each side was trying to prod the other into making the first rash move.

But the first move came from the source of legitimate authority, the prime minister. Pinheiro, chafing at the extent to which he had been let down by his subordinates, admitted on 4 November, 'I don't have the capacity or authority to govern'. Three days later he sent Colonel Neves's commandos to blow up Radio Renascensa's transmitter, and so silence that political gadfly once and for all. Through late October and the first days of November, Pinheiro had been discussing with President Costa Gomes and with Melo Antunes the possibility of removing the indecisive Fabiao and the erratic Otelo from office. By 11 November, the clash between the two groups had come to a head, as Otelo got wind of the talks, and began to boycott meetings of the Supreme Revolutionary Council. 'I am not going to waste my time', he said, 'at meetings devoted to personal attacks and disagreements.'

The end was getting close. Otelo's policy of refusing to enforce the orders of the prime minister had made government of the country impossible, and he knew that before the end of November, his opponents would try to drive him from his post of COPCON commander. He was in touch with the civilian far left groups and tried to co-ordinate a revolutionary strategy. The obvious staging posts for a show of force were the air force bases, where the already heavily left-wing parachute regiments were waiting to move. Otelo never seems to have planned a full-blooded military coup. He lacked the forces to seize power in central Lisbon, much less the north, and he knew it. But control of the strategically placed bases would give him a bargaining card which would make his dismissal almost impossible, and might achieve a new

shake-up of the army hierarchy in Lisbon. The problem was timing.
It was no easy task to organise the undisciplined and disparate forces
behind him, but he wanted to prevent himself being dismissed. As it
happened, events forced his hand as they had General Spinola's eight
months earlier, and like Spinola he may not even have been actively
involved in planning the November uprising.

The Communist party was partly to blame. Always uneasy in his
relationship with Otelo, Alvaro Cunhal was not prepared to gamble
on the flamboyant hero of the far left's chances of avoiding military
confrontation. Limited by his own Stalinist orthodoxy, but still cautious
after his defeats of the summer, Cunhal adopted entirely orthodox
tactics in trying to bring down the government. Strikes were the key
weapon: in a climate of military indiscipline, Cunhal thought that
organised labour had as good a chance as any of emerging the only
survivor from the crumbling social and political structure of Portugal,
and he decided, in the second half of November, on an active campaign
of industrial disruption. At the very least, Cunhal hoped to make it
clear to Portugal's rulers that the country could not be run without the
active consent of the Communists. From his agents, Cunhal knew of
the far left's fevered preparations for armed action. But he prudently
decided not to link his strike campaign to them. Cunhal had few
illusions that the army would ever be subordinate to the Communist
party, whether led by Otelo, Pinheiro or anyone else. Instead, his
party's supporters at a lower level—sergeants, privates—were trying to
spread indiscipline through the ranks, which he hoped would make
Portugal's army incapable of holding power at all.

The labour assault began on 12 November. Some 20,000 construction
workers, among the most militant members of Intersindical because of
the severity of the recession that had hit building in Portugal, marched
on the constituent assembly at Sao Bento, where debates were in
progress. The workers were demanding a 44 per cent increase in their
basic rate of £80 a week, which they described as a 'starvation wage'.
Police were on hand at Sao Bento, but made no attempt to disperse the
demonstrators, who declared that they would surround the palace
until their demands were met. Of senior government members, only
Admiral Vitor Crespo was inside the palace. But journalists and deputies in the assembly were trapped for twenty-four hours. The scene
throughout the afternoon of 12 November was one of relative calm,
punctuated by the cheers of the crowd as a contingent of strikers moved
towards the prime minister's residence across the road from the
palace. COPCON troops made no attempt to stop the demonstrators
as they climbed over the walls and into the gardens, although a contingent of personal guards kept them from entering the residence itself.
But Pinheiro too was trapped. And Cunhal, sensing the kill, ordered

reinforcements to his workers' army up from the farmworkers' strong-holds of the south.

Pinheiro was nothing if not stubborn, and refused to negotiate with the strikers until the following day. He was eventually prevailed upon by persistent telephone calls from President Costa Gomes, who urged surrender, and from Melo Antunes, who argued that an out-and-out confrontation with a large body of workers would be the worst possible way of reasserting his authority. Antunes's backing force under Colonel Eanes, who was waiting quietly in the wings, could not break up a large and so far peaceful demonstration without spilling a great deal of blood, and without revealing the existence of the intervention force before the time was ripe. A civilian counter-demonstration by the democratic political parties was ruled out as too obvious a prelude to open street fighting. That left Otelo, and Otelo flatly refused to come to the prime minister's aid.

Pinheiro, a prime minister besieged in his own home, finally yielded to the strikers' demands in the early morning of 14 November. The workers dispersed with cries of 'Victory! Victory!' The country moved towards an open geographical partition between the two sides. With order apparently unenforceable in the streets of Lisbon, with the left on the ascendant in the south and in the capital, the north seemed to be the last bastion of democracy. In Oporto that same night, eleven people were injured as anti-Communist crowds sacked Communist buildings. In Lisbon the Communists called a mass demonstration on 15 November to celebrate their victory. Most of the moderate military men and the democratic political leaders absented themselves discreetly from the capital for the weekend. Leaders of all three democratic parties met in secret session in Oporto. And on 17 November, 213 non-Communist members of the constituent assembly met in Oporto to discuss transferring their sessions there permanently. As one member put it: 'The mob rules Lisbon. Nobody governs it.'

Only Pinheiro stayed in Lisbon, exhausted and alone. At a large Socialist rally in Oporto, Mario Soares denounced the Communist attempt to 'destroy the sixth provisional government and to set up a dictatorship'. Down in Lisbon they were chanting, 'Vasco, Vasco Vasco will return!' Otelo, jumping on the bandwagon, sent a telegram to the Communist leaders reading: 'I salute this glorious demonstration by the real working people. Otelo is with you.' But the two main leftist groups, the union militants controlled by the Communists, and the army irregulars run by Otelo, still mistrusted each other too much to co-ordinate their activities in the ensuing ten days.

The danger of the country drifting into two armed camps, the north and the south, became sharper with a story that the northern military commander, Brigadier Pires Veloso, was mobilising his troops for a march on the south. A spokesman for Veloso described the rumour as 'nonsense', but left-wing groups jumped at the opportunity of denouncing a 'fascist conspiracy', which they said included the commander of the central military region, Brigadier Franco Charais, and Brigadier Vasco Lourenco, who was becoming a firm favourite to succeed Otelo as military governor of Lisbon. Lourenco, an early protégé of Otelo had become disillusioned with his old boss, and had drifted into Melo Antunes's orbit. As a leader he showed much the same mixture of flamboyance, occasional operational brilliance and rank amateurishness that Otelo did. Few expected that his impending promotion by President Costa Gomes would be anything more than a typically flabby response to the overwhelming pressure among officers to do something about Otelo.

But the quiet man who led the soldiers behind Antunes would not move. Consulted by Antunes the following week, Colonel Eanes insisted that the left had to overreach itself first, as it surely would if Otelo was dismissed. The situation in Lisbon was deteriorating fast; strikes of bakers and canning workers had followed after the successful building workers' strike. Pinheiro, frustrated and tired, acted impetuously. After a cabinet meeting on 20 November, he announced that the government would 'suspend its functions' unless President Costa Gomes, as commander in chief of the armed forces, could guarantee it the backing of the armed forces. 'I am sick of playing children's games,' said Pinheiro. 'I don't like being besieged.' An official statement said explicitly: 'Recent events show that the government, which does not have the armed forces under its jurisdiction, does not have the possibility of effectively assuring normal government activity in certain zones of the country.' Ostensibly directed at the vacillating but powerless figure of the president, Pinheiro was trying to precipitate the left-wing coup attempt that would force Eanes and his men to act. Enough, for the admiral, was enough. It was time for battle, although he could not be certain of the outcome.

Coasta Gomes had the power to dismiss his striking government, which was what the Communists immediately urged him to do. He also had the power finally to fire Otelo. But the following day, 21 November, he characteristically chose a middle course. Otelo was replaced by Vasco Lourenco as military governor of Lisbon, but not as head of COPCON. Under the chairmanship of Costa Gomes, the Supreme Revolutionary Council also empowered Otelo to try to form his 'people's power' movement to replace the elected political parties. Adding insult to this brazen concession to the most anti-democratic left-wing pressures, Ramiro Correia's Fifth Division, responsible for 'cultural dynamisation', was to be revived. Costa Gomes also indicated that the government was to be reshuffled to give

D

the Communists a greater say. This package of contradictions was rounded off with a denunciation of Pinheiro's government for going on strike. The lengths to which Portugal's military chiefs would go to appease the militant factions were illustrated at a passing-out parade for 200 army recruits the same day. The army commander-in-chief, General Fabiao, looked proudly on as they swore, with clenched fists, their own revolutionary oath: 'To fight with all our might, willingly accepting revolutionary discipline, against fascism, imperialism, for democracy, power to the people and the victory of the socialist revolution.'

The Supreme Revolutionary Council was out of touch, that much was clear. Its decisions infuriated both right and left, but it was Otelo's men who took to the streets that Friday evening in Lisbon. As hordes of left-wingers roamed the centre of the capital, Otelo sought out leading members of the Revolutionary Council, and threatened to stage his coup then and there. By morning, Costa Gomes and the councillors had agreed to reinstate Otelo as Lisbon's military governor. The capitulation to the left was complete.

Neither Pinheiro nor the democratic parties could let Costa Gomes get away so easily. At another of the mass demonstrations that had become commonplace in Lisbon's foetid political atmosphere, Mario Soares was in an unusually ferocious mood. For the first time he attacked the president himself for his lack of leadership. 'If the price of freedom is to fight, we will fight,' he told 40,000 cheering supporters. 'Not only were they [the Communists] beaten on 25 April at the polls, they will be beaten with arms as well if they come out on to the streets.'

Surprisingly, the northern military commander, Brigadier Pires Veloso, shared the platform with the Socialist leader. One of Soares's main concerns during those tense November days was to prevent the right-wing soldiers who were becoming Portugal's only hope for democracy from drifting back to their old authoritarian convictions. If the far left was crushed, Soares did not want the far right put in its place. But none of the key army commanders—Pires Veloso in the north, Charais in the centre, Eanes and Neves—showed any sign to Soares of wavering in their commitment to democracy, as long as Soares and Pinheiro for their part held out firmly against the Communists and far left. And this Pinheiro, with his obstinacy, and Soares, with his fingertip grasp of political realities, were intent on doing.

On the evening of 24 November, the far left at last fell into the trap and decided to act. With the president swaying wildly from one side to the other, it was time to put on a display of force. Northern Portugal's increasingly militant farmers had taken a leaf out of the Communists' book, and the same evening blocked all food going to Lisbon along the main northern approaches. Otelo feared that Costa Gomes would

yield to this latest threat, and reverse his decision, putting the
COPCON commander out of a job again. For Otelo it was now or
never. Sure enough, in the early morning Vasco Lourenco was
renominated military governor of Lisbon. The fuse for the far-left
uprising had been lit.

Before dawn that same morning of 25 November, far-left paratroops
moved in to seize the Monsanto air base on the outskirts of Lisbon.
They caught the inmates by surprise and took the deputy air force
chief, General Pinho Freire, prisoner. The paratroops were then taken
by helicopter and tank to three other air bases near the capital, at
Montijo, Tancos and Monreal, which were seized without a struggle.
Unfortunately for the revolutionaries, most of the birds—the aeroplanes
at the bases—had flown, in anticipation of just such a move. In proud
prossession of their somewhat valueless military targets, the rebels
broadcast a demand for the reinstatement of Otelo, who had taken no
active part in the uprising. The revolt appeared to catch the Communists on the hop. Neither RAL-1, Dinis de Almeida's artillery regiment,
nor the pro-Communist Queluz infantry regiment, made any move.

Soon after the bases were seized Eanes's and Neves's troops went
smoothly into operation. Loyalist air force planes buzzed over Lisbon
throughout the day. A force of Neves's commandos moved into
Monsanto, and immediately impressed the rebel paratroops with their
efficiency and discipline. After verbal exchanges between besiegers and
besieged, a round of shooting broke out in the Lisbon suburbs, injuring
three bystanders. When the rebels saw that they were outgunned,
outmanned and outmanoeuvred, they surrendered, some of them
fraternising with the commandos as they came out, and some of them,
in the confusion, managing to escape arrest. The rebels in Monreal put
up no resistance at all after a large crowd of pro-government civilians
had surrounded the base, bringing support to the professional soldiers
who had moved into the area. The rebels at Montijo and Tancos
managed to negotiate with armoured units under Eanes's command
well into the night before surrendering. The unexpected re-emergence
of loyalist troops had taken all of Otelo's supporters by surprise.

In Lisbon, the rebels managed to seize control in the early morning
of the radio and television stations, but they were dislodged by
nightfall. A tenser scene took place outside the presidential palace at
Belem, where by midday a large crowd of extreme left-wingers had
gathered. A contingent of commandos opened fire on the demonstrators, but no one was injured. A few hours later, a larger contingent of
commandos arrived to take control of the military police barracks near
the palace, one of the left's last major strongholds. The commandos
were at one stage caught between two fires, from the military police in
front, and from left-wing civilian snipers behind. But only two men

were killed by the time the left-wingers laid down their arms and surrendered. During the night, loyalist units which had been rushed down from the north by Pires Veloso replaced the weary commandos.

Costa Gomes had called a meeting of the Supreme Revolutionary Council as soon as news of the revolt had reached him. Eanes, who was acting with the authority of a prime minister, regally refused to attend the session, although he had complete operational control of Lisbon. At lunchtime the president declared a state of emergency, banned all demonstrations and ordered a curfew from midnight. By evening, Otelo had been summoned to Belem, and Costa Gomes broadcast to the nation through transmitters beamed from Oporto. Surrounded by moderate ministers, including Pinheiro, Costa Gomes denounced the rebel paratroops as the 'victims of a criminal manipulation'. In the background, Otelo watched despondently, flanked by security men.

11   The professional soldier

Where had Antonio Ramalho Eanes sprung from? The question was to bemuse Portuguese commentators for months afterwards. For a year after the departure of General Spinola, Portugal had had no leader, but had been buffeted about between rival groups of soldiers, none of them strong enough, apparently, to grasp absolute power. Suddenly, out of the ferment, had sprung a leader, a man of few words but backed by disciplined units no one knew still existed, and had cut off Portugal's other more garrulous soldiers in mid-sentence. With his dark glasses and stern, unsmiling face, the newly promoted General Eanes looked almost a caricature of a Latin military dictator. But, like almost everything else about him, his looks were deceptive. When they forced him to take off his dark glasses and wear civilian clothes, to look more democratic, he ended up looking like a mild-mannered bank clerk.

General Eanes came, as do so many prominent Portuguese, from a country district, Alcains in the municipality of Castelo Branco. Like many another boy from a lower-middle-class background, he worked hard to pay his way to go to lyceum, and at the age of seventeen he went to army school. Serious, intensely hard working, and with a mind that was not so much quick as thorough, he was the very model of a modern professional officer. Promotion was fast if unspectacular. At twenty-two he was a sub-lieutenant, and was sent out to Portuguese India, where he became a lieutenant at twenty-four. Returning to Lisbon, he became a captain at twenty-six, and served in Macau in 1962, Mozambique in 1964 and in 1966–8, and in Guinea in 1969. In 1973, at the age of thirty-eight, he became a major. In 1974 he was sent out to Angola.

By then, Eanes had already taken part in the first meetings of the Armed Forces Movement. As an intelligent, widely-read officer, he had misgivings about the country's colonial policy from an early stage, but he was never infected, as some of his colleagues were, by the idealism of those he was fighting. It was not then apparent that the MFA leaders had any particular ideological axe to grind, beyond their doubts about the direction of Portugal's colonial policy, and a sense of professional grievance. Eanes himself greatly admired Spinola's book *Portugal and the Future*, published at the beginning of 1974, outlining a more gradualist colonial approach.

After the Lisbon coup took place, Eanes was recalled from Luanda to Lisbon by Spinola, who considered him a promising young officer and a more trustworthy one than many of the left-wingers on the MFA co-ordinating committee. The major was promoted to lieutenant-colonel and was appointed to the committee running the ministry of social communication. Not a man of many words, he took little part in the political disputes with which the committee was beset, but ran his side of the ministry with an efficiency rare in Portuguese administration then or since. Distrusted by none, he was appointed to the sensitive post of armed forces representative for Portuguese television, and after Spinola's resignation on 28 September had caught him as much by surprise as it did everyone else, he became chairman of the board of directors for Portuguese television.

Eanes was at the time under the direct command of the minister without portfolio responsible for the media, Major Vitor Alves. The major was one of the most sensitive and intelligent figures in the Portuguese leadership, and belonged to the small clique around Major Melo Antunes, the revolution's ubiquitous *éminence grise*. As autumn turned to winter and the stampede to the left began in earnest, Eanes grew more and more doubtful about his ability to control the stream of far-left propaganda being put out by the journalists on Portuguese television. Both he and Alves found themselves struggling to get any news, let alone political broadcasts, on the air concerning the activities of the two embryonic right-of-centre parties, the Centre Democrats and the Popular Democrats. The blacking of news programmes sometimes even extended to Mario Soares's Socialists. With the Antunes group growing ever more alarmed in early 1975 at the direction of events, they began to form links with the Socialist party, and the possibility of an attempt to restore Spinola was canvassed, although Antunes finally preferred the idea of a palace coup to replace prime minister Goncalves and retain President Costa Gomes. Eanes was party to some of the discussions, and forged his first links with the Socialist party at this time, but there is nothing to suggest that he was actively involved in any plotting.

After the 11 March fiasco, Eanes was dismissed as head of Portuguese television. But he denied all charges of having been implicated in the coup and was subsequently exonerated in an official inquiry. The evidence suggests that even at that early stage he had been taken under Melo Antunes's wing and was benefiting from his protection. Antunes and Vitor Alves had both been threatened with expulsion from the Supreme Revolutionary Council, and were only saved through the intercession on their behalf of Admiral Vitor Crespo, the high commissioner in Mozambique. But as Antunes's strength grew through the early summer of 1975, he secured Eanes a post on the general staff of the armed forces. In late summer he was given the job of purging the main military disseminator of far-left propaganda, the Fifth Division.

Throughout the summer of 1975, indeed ever since the departure to exile of his old boss, Eanes had been in touch with Spinola, together with a group of other close associates, among them Lieutenant-Colonel Firmino Miguel, the man Spinola had wanted to make prime minister in 1974 instead of Vasco Goncalves, and Colonel Monteiro Pereira, who had been Spinola's *chef du cabinet*. Spinola was at that time setting up his exile group in Spain, the Democratic Movement for the Liberation of Portugal (MDLP), which had two branches. The first, commanded by Lieutenant-Colonel Santos e Castro, was based in Angola. The lieutenant-colonel was chief adviser to Holden Roberto, head of the National Front for the Liberation of Angola, during the winter of 1975. Santos e Castro was a political moderate, who shared Spinola's commitment to restoring democracy in Portugal.

The second group was based outside Madrid, under the control of Commander Alpoim Calvao, a spectacular commando fighter in Angola, who was more inclined to favour a right-wing government to restore order in Portugal after the traumas suffered under the extreme left. Spinola's *éminence grise* at the time was Manuel Cotta Dias, a former economics minister and head of the governing party in parliament under Marcello Caetano. Cotta Dias, a dry, acerbic man, had close business connections with the exiled denizens of Portuguese banking and industry. Cotta Dias's main objective was to bring Spinola round to accepting that he must act with decision and authority to restore business confidence in Portugal before attempting to hand over power to an elected civilian government.

The exile scene was further crowded by the ELP, the Portuguese Liberation Army, which was always a small group of extreme right-wingers, but one capable of staging spectacular acts, such as the freeing from a prison hospital in Lisbon in the summer of 1975 of the son of Barbieri Cardoso, the former PIDE chief.

The MDLP's most successful operation was the carefully planned anti-Communist uprising in the north, orchestrated by its agents in provincial towns who worked with local Popular Democratic and some Socialist parties. But even at that stage the organisation was extremely loosely federated. Spinola could call himself its leader because no one in Portugal of his prominence would admit they belonged to it. The Portuguese soldiers and party militants whom he considered under his orders, kept in close touch with him but never obeyed him blindly. Indeed, they were more content to follow the political lead set by Melo Antunes. Eanes's task in the summer months became that of knitting together that loose political federation and the military units which he thought were prepared to fight to resist a far-left takeover. Always detached, he showed supreme professional confidence without voicing any open dissent against the political leadership of Melo Antunes. In turn the politicised major considered Eanes to be the ideal of an unambitious professional soldier.

Very few units in the Portuguese army had been left untouched by the general indiscipline, and could therefore be relied upon, although officer support for the organisation being put together by Eanes was growing fast. The one unit whose discipline and courage all soldiers respected was the Amadora commando regiment, headed by the tough, able, and almost completely non-political Colonel Jaime Neves. Neves was a man who could command, but who liked the good life, and did not care to indulge in barrack-room politics. He was under the political sway of Lieutenant-Colonel Soares Carneiro, president of the commando association, which could call on considerable firepower from a large number of ex-commandos—from whose ranks were drawn, incidentally, bodyguards used by the leaders of the democratic political parties. Soares Carneiro was a man with an extremely subtle mind who preferred to hide himself behind the impenetrable façade of the duty-bound professional soldier. Unlike other officers, he never gave press interviews and his contacts with civilian political leaders were extremely rare. He liked to think of himself, through the influence he wielded, as a simple soldier acting as a guardian of the Portuguese people's interests. At the time he favoured democracy in Portugal.

With Soares Carneiro's blessing Jaime Neves agreed to join Eanes's organisation, the newly formed United Military Front (FMU). The Communists, who had the best Intelligence service of the political parties, were not slow in working out what was going on. Three Communist sergeants in the Amadora commando regiment attempted to get Jaime Neves dismissed as regimental commander on a trumped-up charge of plotting a coup in June 1975. Neves appealed to his superior, Otelo de Carvalho, head of COPCON. Otelo and Neves, as two good-living, swashbuckling figures with limited political ideas, however different, had a lot in common. The COPCON chief went down to the Amadora headquarters, to hear the regiment testify its faith in Neves with almost complete unanimity. Otelo himself, under fire from the Communists, was not feeling well-disposed towards the sergeants and, making one of his more disastrous mistakes, reinstated the colonel. Otelo no doubt considered a placated Neves to be less dangerous than a discontented, unjustly dismissed Neves. Otelo must have calculated that the commando chief's dismissal was unlikely to loosen his hold over the loyalties of his men.

Through the hot political summer of 1975 Melo Antunes had an almost impossibly delicate political game to play, and pulling it off was probably the single greatest contribution to democracy of that subtle and Machiavellian political mind. He wanted to stop the drive to the left, but at the same time prevent the hodge-podge of army and civilian groups loosely federated under the umbrella of the MDLP from getting out of his control and sweeping Portugal back to the right, and toppling even him from his pedestal. All the right-wing pressures building slowly but inevitably up against what had happened to Portugal over the previous year had to be channelled to one specific purpose—pulling Portugal out of the grip of the far left—and then be gently and harmlessly released before their momentum drove Portugal back into the arms of a conservative dictatorship. Antunes and Mario Soares both feared they would not be able to control the right. But the northern anti-Communist riots showed how effectively Antunes could play up to the MDLP. He circulated the document of the nine, he carefully orchestrated the campaign against Vasco Goncalves, he played on Otelo's suspicions of Communist intentions, he threatened at length to move north and raise the standard there. It was all a virtuoso display of political bravura, designed to show Spinola and the MDLP that he alone was directing the anti-Communist forces inside Portugal.

But the real crunch came after Vasco Goncalves had been forced from office at the end of August. Costa Gomes was prevailed upon to appoint a friend and sympathiser of Melo Antune, Admiral Pinheiro de Azevedo, as prime minister. The admiral had not been a political animal in the past, and so was an unknown quantity for most officers, including the right. But Antunes's motive was to flummox all sides, and then to swing the main body of the MDLP inside Portugal into supporting the admiral.

The linch-pin of this tactic was Eanes. The industrious lieutenant-colonel was the only man in a position to persuade his operational group, the United Military Front, to take a neutral attitude towards the Pinheiro de Azevedo government. Cotta Dias in Spain could see no advantage from the change of prime minister at all, and made this clear in his conversations with Spinola in Rio de Janeiro. He urged that the MDLP should strike while the iron was still hot, after Goncalves's dismissal, and do away too with the pink Socialism of the Antunes group.

Eanes came round to accepting only part of Melo Antunes's arguments for giving Pinheiro a chance. Eanes was not convinced, and events were to bear him out, that the admiral could govern effectively without the support of the forces in the FMU. He did not believe, as Melo Antunes hoped, that the Communists would quitely give up their attempts to destroy the Pinheiro government. But he and Soares Carneiro did accept that Spinola was a little out of touch across the Atlantic in Rio, and that even as a figurehead he was becoming more of an Aunt Sally for the left than a potential rallying point for the right. Antunes's links with Spinola's organisation had been established in the first place as much to keep an eye on what the old guard was up to as to make use of the forces at its disposal. And now both Eanes and Antunes, for different reasons, saw the advantage in severing any connection with Spinola. By itself, the Spanish exile army commanded by Alpoim Calvao had no prospect of leading a successful attack on Portugal from the outside. And inside Portugal, Eanes and Melo Antunes had the greater loyalty of the men in the civilian organisation of the MDLP, whose summer uprising had proved so much of a success.

So the MDLP fell apart. Spinola was left once more as a general without an army, and his humiliating to-ings and fro-ings between Rio, Madrid and Geneva became all the more frantic, as he sought to re-establish his waning influence. It was a sad end for a vainglorious but essentially democratic and genuinely moderate leader, who had tried to give his best to his country.

Eanes's policy as commander of the FMU over the next two months was to stay well in the background, and wait until the left overreached itself. Antunes favoured an early intervention, to give Pinheiro de Azevedo's government a chance to beat down the challenge from the extreme left and establish itself as a viable Socialist-military government. But Eanes argued that his reserve force could only come into action when it became clear to all Portuguese that the only alternative was the country's disintegration. Eanes claimed he could not act decisively until the left gave him the excuse. To crack down on the extremists in the army, and in particular on Otelo, would, he insisted, be to risk creating popular martyrs. Antunes accepted the argument reluctantly, because he was in no position not to. Pinheiro de Azevedo, in the firing line, was furious that the guarantees of support from the army which Antunes had offered him when he took office as prime minister were not to be fulfilled. He suspended his government's functions on 10 November as much in resigned protest against the FMU's failure to back him as from an acceptance of the fact that he could not go on governing against the wishes of the far left. Pinheiro wanted to precipitate a crisis in which the FMU would have to take action; and he succeeded.

Otelo himself knew of the formation of the FMU from his own Intelligence sources. In September, Vasco Lourenco had bragged to him that the group of nine now had the operational forces to enforce its authority. But, in Otelo's words,

> We could do nothing. 90 per cent of all serving officers have signed the document supporting the group of nine in August. I knew that the game was almost up. Had we been prepared to fight, I am sure

we could have taken Lisbon and controlled the south. We might have been able to hold them for a while, although there are many more units and people in the north—6 million compared to 3 million in the south. But only one military unit in the south was on our side. And I was not prepared to consider the cost in human terms of a civil war.

Otelo was a curious mixture of some of the best Portuguese qualities—he was a realist, a good loser, a humanitarian—coupled with a personal and completely erratic far-left ideology. He was a gambler, and he had lost. Roll on tomorrow; he was still having fun.

Some mystery still shrouds the question of whether the far-left uprising of 25 November was a put-up job to give Eanes and his troops the chance to move in and suppress the far left once and for all. To Otelo it seems clear that Eanes was waiting for it. Earlier in November, 123 officers had left the Tancos base, following a dispute with the Communist-dominated sergeants there. Only five left-wing officers were left. But the air force chief, General Morais e Silva, who had once been considered left-wing but was now moving sharply to the right, took no disciplinary action. On 24 November these truant officers, according to left-wing accounts, rang around the three left-wing strong-holds—the RAL-1 light infantry regiment, the military police and the parachutist regiment—giving them orders in Otelo's name to stage an uprising the following day.

Perhaps the most convincing evidence that the Eanes forces at least had prior knowledge that the uprising would take place was not only that they were ready for action, but that the planes at the Montijo air base, shortly before the rebels took control, had been flown out of harm's way to Oporto, on the orders of Morais e Silva. The air force seemed well prepared for any eventuality. Starting in the early morning of 25 November, loyalist air force planes swept low over Lisbon and Setubal.

There was also the coincidence of the farmers' revolt in Rio Maior. The farmers' confederation, CAP, had all along been closely linked with the civilian arm of the Eanes group. The rally's organisers did not limit themselves to threatening to cut off food, gas and electricity supplies to Lisbon, which made it inevitable that President Costa Gomes would have to take some sort of action; the farmers also set up barricades along the main roads to Lisbon from the north, to prevent left-wing forces being rushed from outlying towns to Lisbon. In the event, none came along the roads, and, as the far-left uprising was crushed, the farmers melted back to their northern smallholdings.

Otelo says he was at home when he heard the news of the uprising on 25 November at 6.00 a.m. Not wishing to be implicated, he stayed there. At 2.00 p.m. he went to COPCON headquarters, and then to

Belem palace to meet President Costa Gomes. All the rest of the day he spent talking to the rebel forces on the telephone, trying to convince them to lay down arms, because they had claimed that the sole purpose of the uprising was to protest against his dismissal as COPCON commander. At 6.00 p.m. the Eanes group moved into action; and by 6.00 a.m. the following morning the last air base had surrendered. Otelo's COPCON troops were all ordered to stay in their barracks. As Otelo puts it, 'Had I known of what was about to happen, my troops would certainly not have still been in their barracks.'

It was the end of Otelo's power, and he knew it. On 26 November, he appeared before the Supreme Revolutionary Council for the last time, to resign from it and to ask to be demoted to the rank of major, before both appointments were taken from him. He was placed under house arrest. With him were the names that had dominated the interminable wranglings of Portuguese politics over the previous eighteen months. General Fabiao resigned at last; the outgoing army chief of staff had been too indecisive a figure to feature in Melo Antunes's plans, and his indecision cost him his career. Admiral Rosa Coutinho, the former Angolan high commissioner, Major Costa Martins, the former labour minister, and Brigadier Eurico Corvacho, the former northern military commander, went into hiding as other left wingers were rounded up. The pro-Communist navy chief, Admiral Figueira Soares, was dismissed. About eighty officers, including Goncalves's former deputy prime minister, Lieutenent-Colonel Arnao Metelo, were arrested. COPCON was disbanded, and its component units were told to take their orders directly from the president.

12   The delivery

General Eanes became army chief of staff, in succession to Fabiao. Melo Antunes was only too well aware how, suddenly, Eanes had become the hero of the hour, how the general was now the undisputed leader of the 'operational' FMU group. Antunes's main hope was that he could still project enough of his powerful political mind to keep the taciturn Eanes broadly behind his goal of a democracy limited by the watchful eye of benevolent socialist soldiers. On 26 November, Antunes was already trying to restore the old balancing act. A continued Communist presence in government, he said was 'essential, even if it is only a small one'.

In their turn the Communists, well forewarned by the Intelligence reports of what was to happen on 25 November, had swiftly disassociated themselves from the far-left uprising. In leaflets already printed by the evening of the same day, the Communists warned that 'the forces of the left would be committing a grave error by overestimating their forces and attempting any desperate act'. But Mario Soares had tried to make some mud stick to the Communist party by attacking this 'vast manoeuvre—an attempt like the coup in Prague in 1968 to try to impose a Communist military dictatorship'. The Socialist leader was irritated by the speed with which Melo Antunes had waded in to try to restore the political balance and prevent the anti-Communist reaction from getting out of hand. Soares even suggested to Eanes and Costa Gomes that the government issue a statement seeking to implicate the Communists in the 25 November coup, to which the latter, who was afraid of losing his own job, agreed.

Within days of Eanes's appointment as chief of staff, it became clear that Melo Antunes had underestimated him. Eanes had been the loyal subordinate, the politically neutral professional officer doing his duty for as long as he needed to be. Now, with the backing of Portugal's disciplined units, he was the strongman, and it was clear that he had done a lot of his own thinking about Portuguese politics. His point of departure was that Portugal's soldiers should get back to the barracks. The attempt at military rule had been bad both for Portugal and for the army. The general pointed out how easy it had been to crush the 25 November uprising because his units 'were commanded by officers with military ethics, who are not mortgaged to political groups and who are not pawned to sects'. Eanes's views were echoed by Jaime Neves, who openly humiliated President Costa Gomes, when the president was 'invited' to meet the commando leader. 'The people's will for pluralism must really be satisfied,' the colonel lectured the president. 'At this moment the commando regiment is not satisfied. It thinks there is much more to be done and is firmly determined to go to the limit.'

Costa Gomes, for whom time as president was running out, pleaded with Melo Antunes for the preservation of the army's role. All the old arguments about the army as the guarantor of the revolution were trotted out in subsequent meetings with Eanes, Jaime Neves and Soares Carneiro. The clash between the two groups first came to a head over the issue of whether the Communists' single member in government should be allowed to stay. At first Antunes was deserted even by his former civilian allies, the Socialists, who could see no merit in the arguments either for keeping the Communists in government or for keeping the soldiers in power. In an interview to the new Lisbon newspaper *Jornal Novo*, Mario Soares said that the Communists should only stay if they repudiated the coup attempt of 25 November, and if they stopped trying to frustrate government policy. The party could not 'have two policies, one for inside the government, and one for outside it'. The civilian pressure was reinforced in demands by both the Popular Democrats and the Centre Democrats for the Communists to be ejected from government.

In the succeeding days, Melo Antunes managed slowly to persuade Soares to share his anxieties about the backlash to the right. The Socialist leader finally agreed to soften on the Communist issue after an intransigent demand for the Communists to be ejected was made by the Popular Democratic leader, Francisco Sa Carneiro, on 4 December. Soares and Sa Carneiro intensely disliked each other, and the latter's former contacts with exiles in Spain had strengthened Soares's suspicion that the Popular Democratic leader was hatching something with the officers now in control. The next day, Soares defended the Communists: 'The influence of the Communist party in the working class cannot be ignored. More than 700,000 people voted for the Communist party and these people cannot be put in a ghetto.' It was the beginning of Soares's new middle of the road policy, of putting an equal distance between himself and the Communists and himself and the right, which was to isolate his party the following year.

Alvaro Cunhal, for the Communists, was offering some of the moderate noises that Soares had demanded. He denied that the officers involved in the 25 November uprising had been his members. 'They were not our militants, nor did they always think like us. At times they caused us great embarrassment.' At a rally in the Lisbon bullring on 7 December, Cunhal told 20,000 despondent supporters— a much smaller crowd than usual—that the uprising had been 'disastrous'. He went on: 'The working masses must understand the new realities; they must understand that our system of alliances and our form of struggle must be revised.' The Communist leader fiercely attacked the extreme left, and told his supporters that 'certain words' had to be pronounced before his party could resume the offensive. In so many words, he admitted that the Russians had urged him to call off his revolutionary tactics. He even said that he would accept the rules of the parliamentary elections next April, provided these were 'truly' free.

The speech satisfied Soares and Antunes, and, more important, Eanes. The Popular Democrats' demand that the Communists be thrown out of the government fizzled out when Sa Carneiro found, at his party's congress in Aveiro in central Portugal, that he had a revolt on his hands. He took the opportunity to accept the resignation from the party of Emidio Guerrero, who had so incompetently supplanted him as its leader in the summer. The PPD minister for social affairs, Jose Sa Borges, also resigned in protest from the party. In cementing his hold over the PPD, Sa Carneiro accepted that its divisions had made it too weak to push its demand for Communist exclusion from the government. The Aveiro congress ended with a ritual condemnation of the Communists, but no further call for their expulsion.

The next few months were to see Melo Antunes grappling to maintain his dwindling influence on Portuguese politics. The foreign minister insisted on 9 December that the army still had a useful role to play in politics: 'If the MFA disappeared and left the country to be ruled by a parliamentary democracy, we would have to conclude Portugal's revolution is finished.' Within days, the old puppet master was being slapped down by the man whose strings he had earlier pulled. At Eanes's instigation, the Supreme Revolutionary Council agreed on 12 December to a revision of the previous year's 'pact' between the political parties and the MFA. Eanes also proposed a seven-point plan to restore discipline to the armed forces, reorganise them, and purge all but the most rigidly non-political officers.

The army commander was as good as his word. The plan slashed the number of servicemen from a colonial peak of 210,000 men to about 26,000 men. 'Revolutionary discipline' was abandoned, and the far-left units ruthlessly purged. General Eanes negotiated with NATO chiefs to give his soldiers a useful role within the alliance, away from domestic politics. The outcome of these deliberations was that NATO agreed to equip a Portuguese air portable brigade for use in southern Europe, and to provide the country with military credits and arms gifts. Eanes intended to professionalise the army and to take it out of politics.

After Eanes's first initiative in mid-December, the Supreme

Revolutionary Council knew that the day-to-day running of affairs in Portugal was out of its hands. Power in the army was now in the hands of the right, straddled by the enigmatic General Eanes, and the right was content for the time being to hand over its power to the civilians.

On 17 December, the first meetings began between the political parties and military leaders to revise the pact. On 30 December, the parties presented their ideas. They insisted on reducing the role of the Supreme Revolutionary Council to that of a mere consultative body for the president. Even then, the council would only be able to give its advice on matters of 'national importance', such as the nomination of a prime minister, the appointment of a defence minister and the dissolution of parliament. The president would be free to accept or reject the council's recommendations. The council would have no independent power to enforce its recommendations except through the president.

The second main recommendation was that the president should be directly elected (not nominated, as agreed under the old constitutional pact) by an electoral college consisting of soldiers and parliamentary representatives. There was some disagreement among the democratic parties themselves on the idea. Some members of the Socialist party, in particular, were worried that direct elections would confer on the president, who was unlikely to be a Socialist, excessive popular legitimacy, and almost irresistible power. The counter-argument, put forward by Mario Soares, was that without a strong, popularly elected executive the army might one day be tempted to take advantage of the divisions between the democratic parties, claiming that no one had the democratic legitimacy to run Portugal.

Predictably enough, the Communists and the MDP presented a negative set of proposals to the five-man military council appointed to study the civilian ideas. The Communists proposed no major revision in the pact signed in April 1975, and were clearly trying to appeal to what lingering authority Melo Antunes and the other left-wingers on the Revolutionary Council, such as Brigadier Vasco Lourenco and Admiral Vitor Crespo, had left. But Antunes had always been a man who survived on his wits alone and lacked a military power base. His arguments still carried a certain weight in the Council of Revolution, for the very good reason that Eanes was beholden to him as the man who first raised him to political eminence. Eanes knew the debt he owed to Antunes and over the next year, as impatience grew among the 'operational' officers of the FMU against the interfering left-wing politicians on the Council of Revolution, Eanes remained its staunch defender. Jaime Neves in particular, who was willing to obey his chief of staff on most things, could not understand why he failed to replace people like Antunes and Lourenco, who were always shooting their mouths off on political and military topics. But Eanes for long stuck to the view that while he profoundly disagreed with Antunes, he was a man who had done Portugal a service during that summer of 1975, and a man better kept voicing his thoughts innocuously on the Revolutionary Council than summarily dismissed.

The divisions between the Antunes group and other officers simmered on without ever reaching crisis dimensions. Portugal had tired of fighting, of confrontations. All sides after 25 November viewed one another warily without wanting to provoke a major conflict. The Communists in the unions occasionally made sabre-rattling noises, but the level of strikes fell dramatically. The Popular Democrats half-heartedly continued their attempt to rid the government of the Communist under-secretary for agriculture, Antonio Bica, but were too preoccupied with their own divisions to have much effect. The ELP, it seemed, was still sporadically active, planting bombs that, in Portuguese fashion, never killed anyone. On 11 January Portugal's farmers gave the government three weeks to start rolling back the excesses of agrarian reform, and then, after vague assurances from Eanes, who was increasingly acting as an unofficial chief executive, called off their threat of a food blockade or a go-slow. Portugal's growing army of refugees from Angola—the *Retornados*—proved a potential threat to law and order, and there were occasional explosions of violence. Equally, there was the danger of a backlash from the Portuguese themselves, who were getting tired of subsidising the retornados, and tired of the different standards of morality that they brought to Portugal. One old man was beaten to death at the funeral of a murder victim because bystanders suspected him of being a retornado. But after the sudden display of 25 November, it seemed that most Portuguese had gratefully rushed back under the shelter of respect for law and order.

In revolutionary-weary Portugal, Antunes and his fellow radicals could count on little popular sympathy for their attempt to keep some hold on power, and they fell back on force of argument alone. Antunes and Vasco Lourenco persuaded Eanes to modify his call for a total army withdrawal from office, when the soldiers presented their first set of constitutional propsals to the political parties on 15 January. The Supreme Revolutionary Council's power was to some extent reasserted: under a new draft the council was to be given a veto over the president's choice of prime minister. The president was also called upon to preside over the council. Rightly suspicious, the parties asked whether this last stipulation meant that the president had to be an army man. Soares roundly declared on 18 January that 'the new proposal is anti-democratic and consecrates military guardianship over our political life'. Four days later, Sa Carneiro slated the proposals as tantamount to 'military dictatorship'.

Antunes struck back by getting the Supreme Revolutionary Council to issue a statement condemning the civilian parties' irresponsibility. But the issue was already out of his hands. By losing the support of Mario Soares, Antunes had given General Eanes the perfect opportunity to step in on behalf of democracy. Eanes personally consulted the party leaders, and privately assured Sa Carneiro that the powers of the Revolutionary Council would be shorn in the next set of proposals. In exchange both Sa Carneiro and Mario Soares accepted that they would recommend to the other parties the choice of a soldier as president. That was not the concession it appeared. Both had independently decided that only a soldier could give the kind of background stability needed for the survival of a democratic government over the next few years.

On 10 February, the new proposals were presented to the political parties. At the same time Eanes, who had been strongly influenced by Sa Carneiro's arguments, went to see President Costa Gomes to ask for some sort of dilution of the Communists' role in government. The result was a government announcement splitting the Communists' only ministry—the ministry of social infrastructure, into two—one to handle public works, the other to run housing, building and urban planning. The Communists' Alvaro Veiga de Oliveira retained only the public works side.

The victory of the democratic parties, spearheaded at this stage by Sa Carneiro, was almost complete. Antunes's last rearguard action was to try and insert a preamble into the new agreement between the parties and the soldiers which insisted on Portugal's total commitment to Socialism and the army's role in guaranteeing this. Soares was in two minds about whether to accept the proposal, but Sa Carneiro and the Centre Democratic leader, Diogo Freitas do Amaral, were adamant that it should be struck out. On the evening of 25 February, Eanes removed the proposal from the army draft, and the following day a new pact was signed rescinding the pact of April 1975. It gave the Revolutionary Council power only to give its opinion on laws passed in parliament, and to pass them back for further consideration. The army's only safeguard—and that depended on the president being a soldier—was to insist on widespread powers for the president, including the right to appoint the prime minister after consultation with the political parties, and to veto legislation, although this could be overridden by a two-thirds majority of the assembly.

The signing ceremony, under which the parties regained the powers they had been forced at gunpoint to give up the year before, was especially poignant as the Communists were this time the only ones unhappy with the pact. Alvaro Cunhal kept clear of the signing ceremony, but the party's parliamentary leader, Octavio Pato, who was considered less of a hardliner, turned up to witness the formal defeat of the party's aims over the previous years. He expressed dissatisfaction with the pact:

> The lack of democratic experience for many years has resulted in rivalries and incomprehension over the past 22 months. This fact makes it inadvisable for the armed forces to continue to play an associate role, even if temporary, in the construction of a new society.

But the man who controlled those armed forces, Ramalho Eanes, didn't agree, and Pato signed the pact.

President Costa Gomes, corklike as ever, was there to watch over the exact reversal of the process he had presided over the previous year. 'The armed forces do not want to reserve for themselves a significant share of the political power. On the contrary, we want to restore it back to the civilian parties chosen by popular will,' he said without the flicker of a smile as he ate the words he had pronounced in April 1975.

Melo Antunes's wholesale defeat left him in an exposed position; and even his friends knew it. The young air force chief General Morais e Silva, once a friend of Otelo, then of Antunes, now began to try and put a clear distance between himself and the sinking major. On 2 March, when new recruits were sworn in at a Lisbon barracks, Morais e Silva tried to echo conservative fears: 'Present circumstances lead to the conclusion that certain forces opposed to democracy will not accept electoral defeat calmly.' The air force general warned that 'some desperate manoeuvre' might be used to defer or to cancel the legislative assembly elections in April. He referred to 'certain elements of the military, dissatisfied for one reason or another'.

Morais e Silva was aiming carefully at Antunes, whose struggle to preserve his power had now taken the form of listing procedural reasons why the legislative assembly elections might have to be postponed. Antunes's strategy was to try and write into the constitution the same cast-iron guarantees that the army should have the power to intervene to preserve Socialism in Portugal if necessary that he had failed to get into the pact between the army and the political parties. In his view the general election must not take place until the constituent assembly had made the necessary alterations to the constitution. The process should not be rushed.

Soares broadly agreed with Antunes's attempt to write Socialism into the constitution, but wanted this to be seen as a civilian, not a military initiative. And the Socialist leader strongly disagreed with Antunes's suggestion that the elections be put off while parliament thoroughly debated the constitutional clauses. By this time the

Socialist leader had an almost religious faith in not postponing elections beyond their deadlines, for fear that they might be cancelled altogether. On 18 March, Antunes came into the open and suggested to the Revolutionary Council that the elections be postponed. The following day, under fire from right-wing officers, who urged his immediate dismissal from the council, he had to cancel a scheduled trip to Sweden, and argue his case with Eanes, who was holding the ring between the two sides. At a meeting of the Revolutionary Council on 24 March, Eanes said that Antunes should stay on the council, but insisted that the elections should go ahead as planned. Eanes was being loyal to his former patron, but unwavering in his course of action. The issue was decided, even if adding the finishing touches to Portugal's constitution might shorten the election period.

Soares now had a potentially tricky task. To get the Socialist guarantees rushed through the constituent assembly, he needed the support of the Communist party against the Centre Democrats and the Popular Democrats. Because time was short, the Socialists had to make open overtures to Alvaro Cunhal, which could, in the prevailing climate of fierce anti-Communism, be electorally dangerous. It was at this time that Soares and his chief lieutenants worked out a strategy that was to govern their actions and to dog Portuguese democratic stablility over the following year. They resolved that a temporary accommodation with the Communists must be offset by a firm undertaking never to enter a coalition government with the party. The electorate must be in no doubt that the Socialists were as anti-Communist as any other party.

But this uncompromising attitude would hardly go down well with the Socialist left. However clearly they agreed with Soares that the Communists were not to be trusted politically, the party's social aims were undeniably more progressive than those of the conservative alternatives, the Centre Democrats and the Popular Democrats. In order to assuage the left, Soares had to give the further pledge that his party would not enter into coalition with either of the other two parties. The result was a formula for instability. Soares could argue that his stubborn one-party approach lent credibility to the Socialist claim that they would emerge as a much strengthened party in the elections. But he knew as well as anyone that they would be lucky to keep their losses to a minimum, in a country which since the summer had been swaying away from the left. The 'no coalition' pledge, which was to be made repeatedly during the election campaign, was popular with most of the rank and file in the party, because it ensured that all government posts and the patronage machine would go to the Socialists if they won. But it arose primarily from the tactical need to keep the party equidistant between the right-wing parties who were disliked by

Soares's own leading lieutenants, and the Communist party, which was disliked by the electorate.

With Communist support, the left-wing provisions of the constitution were passed by the end of March. The Socialists' most vigorous critics then were in the Centre Democratic party, who argued passionately that a constitution existed to safeguard democracy, not to safeguard a particular political dogma. When on 2 April the constitution was finally approved by the constituent assembly, Freitas do Amaral instructed his party to oppose it. They were the only ones: the Communists and the Socialists approved, while the Popular Democrats accepted it reluctantly.

It was, by any standards, an unusual document. The first article stated boldly: 'Portugal is a sovereign republic based on the dignity of the human being and on the will of the people and entrusted with its transformation into a society without classes.' Article 2 committed the country to 'assuring the transition to Socialism through the creation of conditions for the democratic exercise of power by the working classes'. Under Article 3 'the Armed Forces Movement, as a guarantor of the democratic conquests and the revolutionary process, participates, in alliance with the people, in the exercise of sovereignty under the terms of the constitution'. Article 10 insisted on 'the collectivisation of the main means of production'. Article 55 guaranteed the right of worker participation in industry. Pollution control, agrarian reform and nationalisation were also enshrined in the constitution. Article 273 gave the Portuguese armed forces 'the historic mission of guaranteeing the conditions which permit a peaceful transition to democracy and Socialism'.

The constitution was clearly intended to limit the freedom of action of any non-Socialist government elected to power in Portugal, although it was vague enough to make the enforcement of constitutional law difficult. But it was largely democratic, and the uneven Socialist and military bits around the edges were probably the least that could be expected from a country which had narrowly escaped dictatorship by the far left.

The other political parties failed at first to realise the depth of Soares's commitment to go it alone as the price for getting his Socialist constitution through. Sa Carneiro hoped that the Popular Democrats would emerge as the largest single party in the elections, and was keeping his options open for an alliance either with the Socialists or with the Centre Democrats, whichever party would give the government a majority in parliament. Freitas do Amaral considered a coalition with the Popular Democrats was likely in the event that the two parties could command a majority in parliament. But in the likelier event that they couldn't, he was prepared to consider a coalition with the Socialists. Opinion polls suggested that the Centre Democrats would gain substantially; and, as leader of Portugal's conservative party, Freitas do Amaral hoped to join the Socialists in squeezing the ideologically fuzzy Popular Democrats out of the middle of Portuguese politics.

A personal element also entered the Centre Democrats' calculations: Freitas do Amaral and particularly his deputy, Amaro da Costa, got on much better than Sa Carneiro did with the Socialist leader. And neither of the two conservative parties' leaders believed Soares could go it alone if the Socialists were still the largest party after the elections. They underestimated the stubbornness and self-confidence of the man who was fast becoming the hero of the Socialist parties of Western Europe.

Portugal's second election campaign in a year started on 4 April. There was less public response than there had been in the previous one, but meetings were well attended and the party leaders had become better known. Mario Soares, whose national publicity was unrivalled by the other leaders, drew the biggest crowds, and Alvaro Cunhal, who after his reverses in the north stuck to safe ground in Lisbon and and the south, managed still to command large audiences of the Communist faithful. Both the Popular Democrats and the Centre Democrats drew large crowds at their rallies in the north, and only occasional repetitions occurred—in the Lisbon area—of the attacks by left-wing demonstrators that had driven the Centre Democrats virtually underground in the previous election.

The resurgence of the CDS was the main feature of the campaign. Freitas do Amaral and Amaro da Costa made an effective duo at party rallies; so, too, did their independent supporter, General Galvao de Melo, who appeared in bullrings up and down the country. The CDS stronghold was the north east of the country, particularly around Galvao de Melo's home town of Viseu. And the general's eye for the dramatic won him widespread person support. On 5 April he visited the Communist stronghold of Beja in the Alentejo, two days after rioting Communists had killed a man and fourteen others had been injured. He was heavily guarded by troops sent by the southern military commander, Brigadier Pezarat Correia, and only about 300 people risked turning up at the meeting; but by his bravado Galvao de Melo won the headlines.

The resurgence of the Centre Democrats soon became obvious to both the Socialists and the Popular Democrats. Soares abandoned his rosy forecast of an overall majority early in the campaign, and insisted his party would do well to win as much as it had last time. Sa Carneiro, always a difficult, intellectual, somewhat remote personality, was failing to win converts. The Portuguese Communists provided the only real issues in the election, by appealing to the Socialists to join a popular front, which the latter party indignantly refused to do, and by charging that a concurrent NATO exercise in the Atlantic was interference in the election, which seemed a little far-fetched. Economic issues, which dominated people's anxieties throughout the election, were hardly touched upon by the major parties. The Socialists talked about consolidation of the economic order, and neither of the Conservative parties talked about any dramatic rollback in the economic changes since 1974, although they both argued that the private sector should be allowed to survive. Only the Communists and a motley collection of extreme left-wing parties continued to champion the claims of Portuguese workers, but by now that message only appealed in the more heavily industrial areas of Oporto and Lisbon, and in the south.

On polling day there were fears that the politically weary Portuguese would abstain in large numbers. But although turnout was down on the year before—from 93 per cent to 83 per cent—it was still respectable by southern European standards, and high by northern European standards. The votes showed a modest decline by both the Socialists—from 38 per cent to 35 per cent; and the Popular Democrats—from 27 per cent to 24 per cent; and the doubling of the Centre Democratic vote from 7 per cent to 16 per cent. The Communists picked up some votes from the Portuguese Democratic Movement, which was not running this time, and which had urged its supporters to vote for Cunhal. But the vote of the two parties together fell from 18 per cent to 14 per cent. The result confirmed a Portuguese multiparty system in which no party came anywhere close to getting an absolute majority.

A relieved Soares went on television after the results were announced to repeat his intransigent election pledge that the Socialists would coalesce with no one—brave words from the leader of a party which had won only two-fifths of the seats in parliament. Sa Carneiro's disappointment at failing to gain from Portugal's swing to the right was obvious, and criticism at his authoritarian, remote style of leadership was renewed within the party. Sa Carneiro hoped that the next government would be a coalition between his party and the Socialists, possibly including the Centre Democrats as well, but Soares objected that the Communists should not be left alone in opposition. An elated Freitas do Amaral hinted that he would be prepared to do a deal with the Socialists over the Popular Democrats' heads.

The parliamentary puzzler gave a boost to Melo Antunes's argument that politics could not be left to the politicians. Any government, he urged before the Revolutionary Council, must have army members to render it more stable. He preferred a government which included

Socialists, Communists and soldiers. Under the new constitution, Portugal's first democratic government was not scheduled to come into being until the presidential elections, which had been fixed for June. But Antunes favoured immediate action to create a government to consist of what he called the 'majority of the left'. Sa Carneiro looked for a time like obliging him by threatening to pull the Popular Democratic ministers out of the government, ostensibly because the Communists were still represented there, but in fact as a protest against the Socialist refusal to consider a coalition. In what was becoming a habit, Eanes and Costa Gomes persuaded Sa Carneiro to withdraw his threat, after gaining nothing.

The parliamentary stalemate plunged the parties into a furious round of politicking for the next round of elections—for Portugal's presidency—which were likely to decide the complexion of the next government. The presidential manoeuvring had actually been going on for some time. The three democratic political parties had accepted the principle that the president should be a soldier, for three reasons: first, if the civilian parties had put in rival candidates, bitter inter-party wrangling would have ensued, which might have provoked an army intervention. Second, a soldier president was part of the deal by which the army had been reconciled to its withdrawal from politics. Third, a democratically elected soldier president would probably carry more authority in keeping the army out of politics.

The question was, which soldier? As early as January, Freitas do Amaral had mooted the name of Ramalho Eanes as the obvious choice. He had the support and respect of the soldiers who mattered—the operationals from the FMU. And as far as anyone could judge, Eanes was committed to democracy—indeed had been instrumental in getting the army out of politics. Eanes's earlier links with the Socialists would make him acceptable in that quarter. Sure enough, Soares himself had come round to the view that Eanes, however conservative underneath, was the best guarantor of the army's neutrality. The trouble was that Eanes didn't want to run.

Eanes was a professional soldier who preferred planning operations to the intricate machinations of party politics, in which he did not want to get involved. He believed he should stay in the background, looking after the army, which could be used in the last resort if Portuguese democracy was threatened. He had never actively campaigned for any kind of elective office in his life, and his modest, mechanical public image hardly seemed adapted to the task. Above all, his colleagues in the army did not want him to run. Colonels Neves and Carneiro admired him as a soldier, and opposed him compromising himself in politics. They strongly urged him to stay out.

Antunes seized his opportunity. His first choice for president was

Costa Gomes, whose views, when they weren't bending to the political wind, were fairly close to his own. But Costa Gomes had been on too many sides; Antunes soon realised that Costa Gomes would meet with the active hostility of many senior officers, including some of Antunes's own supporters, such as Brigadier Vasco Lourenco, commander of the Lisbon military region. Antunes's second choice was the existing prime minister, Admiral Pinheiro de Azevedo, whose views were left of centre. Pinheiro had won the admiration of Mario Soares; and although lacking a power base in the army was nevertheless looked on with a certain affection for his straightforwardness by most military men. To Soares also, the choice of the admiral seemed the obvious one.

The right-wing parties were not to be outdone. Freitas do Amaral persisted in his conviction that Eanes should continue to be pressurised. But the Centre Democrats began to canvass the chances of General Galvao de Melo, whose personality might count for much during an election campaign. Sa Carneiro's choice was Brigadier Pires Veloso, the commander of the northern military region, whom the Popular Democratic leader incorrectly identified as the most powerful of the operational FMU commanders (Neves and Soares Carneiro were). Veloso played reluctant, but didn't turn down the offer as flatly as Eanes had.

The sudden proliferation of rival candidates convinced Soares that it was essential that Eanes run with the backing of the three main parties. In a meeting between the two men in April, Soares argued that only Eanes could avert a woundingly divisive presidential campaign. Eanes was not convinced, and suggested that Soares himself run, a suggestion that the Socialist leader turned down as unrealistic. But Eanes was reluctant to reconsider. Soares told the other party leaders what he had done, and, on 2 May, Sa Carneiro, sensing the way the wind was blowing, decided to get in first by announcing his party's support for an Eanes candidacy.

Sa Carneiro's jumping the gun mightily irritated Soares, but it did at least bring the issue to a head. On 4 May, Eanes, after careful consideration, told the Revolutionary Council that he would stand in the elections 'only if it is imperative, and only in those circumstances'. Jaime Neves expressed bitter disappointment, and Eanes's choice marked the beginning of a rift between the two men, which was not to come into the open until much later. But on 12 May, after Freitas do Amaral pledged CDS support behind Eanes, Mario Soares met the army commander and announced his own party's endorsement of the reluctant candidate. On 14 May, with the backing of parties which had won almost three-quarters of the vote in the parliamentary elections, Eanes at last declared that he would run.

Pires Veloso, left high and dry by the Popular Democrats' sudden switch of allegiance, immediately pulled out of the race. Galvao de Melo hesitated a little longer, then decided his personal constituency had disappeared. A crestfallen Antunes urged Pinheiro de Azevedo to stay in the race, and the admiral, who had no small regard for his own talents, decided to follow the major's advice. 'Democracy in Portugal does not permit presidential elections with only one candidate,' said Pinheiro de Azevedo bravely on 12 May. 'I am going to act so that the presidential elections will be carried out with at least a minimum of national and international dignity. And that will only come if there are two candidates.' With his main political prop, the Socialists, backing his opponent, Pinheiro's chances were small. They depended on a much longer period in the public eye than Eanes had had in six months as a shadowy chief of staff.

Third into the field was a surprise: the Communists decided to run their own candidate. He was the only civilian in the field, an irony in view of the party's former support for continued military intervention in Portugal's domestic politics. On 18 May, Octavio Pato, the party's parliamentary leader, was presented as a runner at a press conference. Journalists asked him if this meant he was shortly to supplant Alvaro Cunhal, who was sitting beside him, as party leader. Although Pato denied this, it was clear that his public pulling power was being tested. President Costa Gomes also announced at the last minute that a committee was collecting signatures asking him to run, but no one rushed to his banner to endorse him. The president had just lost a libel case against the editor of the satirical paper *O Diabo*, which had lampooned him for changing with 'the political winds' and 'the final fault' that 'you are ugly'. On second thoughts, Costa Gomes, unlamented, decided to stay out.

The last candidate to come in was Otelo Saraiva de Carvalho, drafted by the far-left popular power groups. There had been doubts whether Otelo would be allowed to stand, as he had been arrested briefly in January, and then put under restricted arrest in his modest flat in the working class suburb of Oeiras outside Lisbon, on condition that he made no political declarations. But the government decided to relent rather than victimise him, and the colourful major returned again to the political stage.

He was, he told journalists, 'not a candidate of any party but of the people'. Otelo's campaign was from the first a typical display of showmanship, which left the rest of the earnest, plodding field well behind in the publicity stakes. He claimed to have been responsible for, and implied that Eanes played no part in, the 1974 coup. He attacked the events of 25 November as 'an enormous machination designed to deviate from the line of purity imposed upon it [the revolution] by the working classes and generous and progressive military men'. 'Maybe,' he remarked, on another occasion, 'I am some kind of Robin Hood.'

His easygoing, attractive personality, all bluster and humour and political ingenuousness, gave the campaign its colour and won the support of many Portuguese fed up with the constitutional semantics of political debate over the previous eighteen months. Nobody took Otelo seriously politically, but they warmed to the man. And some of the Communist party's most dogged supporters, who for years had turned out for the national figure of Alvaro Cunhal, could not be pulled in to support the uninspiring Pato. Otelo was a good guy, a champion of the workers and they liked him. The major's campaign got off to an enthusiastic start on 29 May, when two trainloads of supporters chugged north to Oporto to a tumultous welcome. The major railed at international capitalism and the bourgeoisie at whistle stops along the way. If crowds decided elections, he would surely have won. General Eanes commented wryly that if Otelo de Carvalho should win the election, he, Eanes, would leave the country.

But Eanes knew his victory was certain. The only danger was that Otelo on the one hand, and Pinheiro on the other, might between them win enough votes to deny him an absolute majority. In that case he would have to fight a run-off election with his leading rival, which most Portuguese expected to be Pinheiro. Pinheiro's final plain talking, however, only succeeded in losing him votes. On 26 May, he declared: 'It is up to America whether Communists could be allowed into government in Portugal. As long as the United States remains intransigently opposed, I don't see how it's possible.' Pinheiro's aim was both to be frank and to make his candidacy more attractive to the Americans. But Eanes, widely considered the Americans' first choice for president, jumped in to play the nationalist tune and stress his independence from United States pressure:

> That's the admiral's opinion. I have to say that Portugal belongs to one of the blocs, NATO, and fully respects the agreements that derive from it. But it does not accept any interference. Neither, as far as I know, are countries like the United States interested in supervising Portugal's internal affairs.

Pinheiro's campaign drifted from then on from one disaster to another, as he charged the armed forces with a 'conspiracy' to foist Eanes as a one-party candidate on Portugal, when many of Eanes's army friends had expressly tried to dissuade him from running in the face of the political parties' determination to draft him as a candidate. On 3 June, Pinheiro threatened to withdraw from the campaign, saying it would be a 'miracle' to go on campaigning 'without any kind of support'. By 7 June, he had changed his mind, and decided to hand over most of his duties as prime minister to the interior minister, Commander Almeida e Costa. On 24 June, after three weeks of frantic campaigning and small crowds, Pinheiro collapsed in Oporto with a serious heart attack. Under Portugal's election law, if Pinheiro died before the election, it would have to be postponed. In the event, the admiral recovered. But his fiasco of a campaign ensured that the candidate from whom he might have won votes, General Eanes, stayed at the top.

Eanes's campaign was typical of the man. He shunned any pretence at demagoguery. His speeches were dully delivered, to the point. In his meetings with the press he refused to indulge in the invective or personal mud-slinging that they had come to expect of other candidates. On television he was clipped and brief and cold. But in his walkabouts he showed an earnestness, a genuine interest in talking to ordinary people and seeking their views, that endeared him to his supporters. He shed his uniform for unassuming civilian clothes and his dark glasses for clear ones. He never joked, rarely smiled.

The three democratic political parties pulled out all the stops to get their voters out. Indeed they vied with one another to impress on the candidate who his strongest supporters were, and to impress on the electorate that they were the president's party. And although the crowds were smaller than in previous parliamentary elections the by now well-established party machines ensured large pro-Eanes rallies in the closing days of the campaign. He was treated with sympathy and respect by the crowds; he seemed to be the political novice, not they.

On 27 June, a still impressive 75 per cent of Portuguese voters turned out for their third election in fourteen months. Eanes trounced his opponents with 61 per cent of the vote, some 10 per cent short of the total won in April by the parties backing him, but way past the 50 per cent most people expected. Otelo pipped Pinheiro for second place with 16 per cent to the admiral's 14 per cent, and Pato came a desultory third with 7 per cent. Pinheiro sank into obscurity, Pato into the shadows behind Alvaro Cunhal, who for the time being had demonstrated that there was no popular alternative to his leadership of the Communist party. Otelo reverted to the terms of his conditional freedom. The result was the final proof, if one were needed, that the Portuguese were a politically mature people.

The character of the new presidency was rammed home to Portuguese by Eanes at his press conference on the morrow of his election victory. No frivolous celebrations for him. He told reporters that 'insurrection and illegal activities will not be tolerated', that the Communists in southern Portugal would be 'neutralised', and that

Otelo's 'people's power' groups should behave themselves or 'we shall have an adequate answer so that democracy will be defended'.

On 14 July, Ramalho Eanes was driven in a motorcade from his new presidential residence at Belem palace to the national assembly where, in incongrous full military uniform, he was sworn in as Portugal's first democratic president in half a century. He repeated his call for law and order: 'We must eliminate a climate of anarchy, which can only lead to misery and dictatorship . . . any attempts to create parallel powers rooted in activities of an insurrectional character will not be tolerated.' His election, he said, 'was the result of a long and painful road of resistance by the Portuguese people to oppression'. And he summed up his own hopes and fears for democracy's survival:

> Democracy in Portugal is possible, and being possible it has to be viable. Each day the nation has a clearer awareness of the difficulties that threaten. It is well known that irresponsibility and incompetence —often using the names and interests of the workers—advance largely in the field of economic irrationality . . . but certainly not to democracy and much less to socialism. . . . Exploitation will not be allowed to return, or to continue where it still exists. But economic recovery will not be achieved in any way at the cost of the legitimate rights of the workers.

The words might have been General Spinola's two years earlier. A discarded and dejected Costa Gomes watched his intense young successor being sworn in. The pendulum had swung from extreme right to extreme left and was now moving back to the centre. Whether it would settle there, or go the whole way back, no one could tell.

Eanes's first political act was to appoint Mario Soares as prime minister on 16 July, as promised before the election. But he was careful to emphasise that he had no 'personal undertaking' with the Socialists, and that he would not force the Popular Democrats to support them in parliament. His attitude was that, as president, it was his duty to ask the leader of the largest party to form a government which could command a majority in parliament for its programme; if Soares failed, he would have to look for support as leader of a coalition.

Over the next few days Soares sounded out the other parties' attitudes to his government, but flatly refused to do any sort of coalition deal with them. The prime minister designate was banking on two things to keep his government alive. First that the right-wing parties would never find common cause on which to defeat him; on most of the issues that the right could muster a majority in parliament against him, Soares reasoned that the Communists would vote with the Socialists; only if they abstained or voted against him would his government go down. Second, Soares trusted in the will for democratic survival of the two conservative parties. If his government was brought down too quickly, and Portugal embarked on a new phase of unstable political manoeuvring, the worst claims about democratic politics made by impatient military men over the past two years would be confirmed. If Sa Carneiro and Freitas do Amaral wanted Portugal's democracy to survive, they would have to let Soares live. Sure enough, they gave Soares their grudging agreement not to try to bring the government down immediately after 20 July.

Soares rapidly finished the process of putting a cabinet together. Of the 17 ministers he nominated, 11 were Socialists, 3 were independents, and 2 were officers. The two officers, whom he chose with Eanes's agreement, were the defence minister, a post the army insisted on retaining for itself, and the minister of the interior, which was a peace-offering to the soldiers. Lieutenant-Colonel Firmino Miguel, Eanes's close friend and Spinola's thwarted nominee two years earlier for the post of prime minister, got the defence job. Miguel held moderately left-wing views and had been one of the link men with the Socialist party in setting up the operational group of FMU officers before 25 November. Lieutenant-Colonel Costa Bras got the job of minister of the interior.

Soares's economic team was weak. As minister of finance he nominated Henrique Medina Carreira, a lawyer who knew little of economics. Antonio Sousa Gomes, a former company manager, became minister of economic planning. The minister of labour was Marcelo Curto, a meticulously dressed man with a carefully groomed leonine beard, who had a reputation in the party as a left-wing firebrand, which soon melted away. The minister of industry was Walter Rosa, a tried and experienced Socialist politician who was a close friend of Soares. Lopes Cardoso stayed at the ministry of agriculture, which was a conciliatory gesture by Soares to the left, one he was later to regret. The minister of commerce and trade was an experienced and able young economist, Antonio Barreto. The minister of education was Sottomayor Cardia, a mild-mannered ex-Communist. The Secretary of state for information ('Social Communication', as it was still called in Portugal) was Manuel Alegre, a poet who had played a crucial part in the discussions between Soares, Antunes and the Eanes group. On the evening of 23 July, Portugal's first constitutional government was sworn in. And Soares gave an Eanes-style inaugural address in which he painted a black picture of Portugal's unemployment, low investment, urban filth, drugs and prostitution.

On that sombre note, the twenty-seven-month pregnancy of Portuguese democracy was ended: with its own elected president and prime minister, Portugal's democracy had been born.

13   A revolution's hangover

For his first six months in office, Mario Soares exhorted while Portuguese democracy burned. In September, he gave a sombre and realistic portrayal of the state of the economy. Portugal's annual trade deficit was running at $2000 million, its annual budget deficit at $1000 million, and its foreign debt at over $2000 million. The terms of trade showed that if anything Portugal's competitiveness was declining.

But bleak as was the picture he painted, Soares could not pursue concrete objectives: his party was divided on economic policy. The left, against which Soares was taking an increasingly tough line, opposed any measure aimed at reducing consumption. Soares's new finance minister and minister of economic planning believed that Portugal could escape economic recession only by a dash for growth. Monetary contraction of the economy, they argued, would kill off all hopes for a revival at a time when a quarter of the Portuguese workforce was unemployed, and when so much of Portugal's industrial capacity was under-utilised, or not used at all. Expansion was the answer: and what better to generate expansion than state investment. The state now controlled the entire banking sector, industries producing 24 per cent of the country's value added and accounting for 45·5 per cent of total investment.

Portugal's foreign creditors had been arguing for devaluation; the escudo was palpably over-valued, and had been sustained by the selling of Salazar's large foreign exchange reserves, which had now come to an end, and by borrowing against his gold reserves, which were still worth $2 billion. This policy of, as it were, consuming capital to pay for current needs had shielded most Portuguese from the effects of their rulers' gross economic profligacy over the previous two years. The economic ministers, Medina Carreira and Sousa Gomes, were both too worried by the effect of a devaluation on prices to consider it, especially as local elections were looming. The trade gap would have to be made up, they argued, by boosting exports and clamping down on imports. Money growth, they noted, had not been excessive—under 20 per cent in 1975/76—so a further turn of the monetarist screw would solve nothing.

Neither minister had had much experience of economics, as their critics often observed. But Medina Carreira and Sousa Gomes's arguments were supported by some of the best economists in Portugal, including Vitor Constancio, who had become deputy governor of the Bank of Portugal, and an ubiquitous economic troubleshooter, Vasco Viera de Almeida, who was then acting as a kind of roving financial ambassador for Portugal. Where the government's ideas seemed most vulnerable to attack was in its hopes that the state sector would lead to an investment recovery. The nationalised industries were largely divided into two groups: the big monopolies—formerly run by firms like Cuf, and the Champalimaud and Espiritu Santo families, in areas like shipbuilding and cement manufacture—which had been respon- sible for the economic growth of the late 1960s; and a host of small firms, usually taken over by workers, then nationalised, or rather salvaged from bankruptcy, by the state.

The first group had over-expanded in the early 1970s, often on the very shaky credit bases allowed them by the banks, which in many cases were controlled by the same large holding companies. The world recession and the contraction in world demand had hit them particu- larly badly. The crisis in world shipbuilding and the new competitive- ness of Japanese shipyards had struck a severe blow at the foreign currency earnings of Portuguese shipbuilding, and in particular at the massive new yard at Setenave built by the de Mello family on the huge Sado estuary, near Setubal, south of Lisbon. Setenave continued— barely—to make a profit by diversifying swiftly into ship-repairing. But it was a typical case of the overexpansion of the large European companies taken over by the state in 1975.

To their credit, successive Portuguese governments used a light hand in the running of the big nationalised companies. Setenave's manage- ment was typical. The chief shareholder, Jorge de Mello, had left the country in 1975, and was replaced by an able member of his old board, Hugo Fernando de Jesus. The new board had to seek the government's approval for floating large foreign loans, and submitted its accounts and general investment programme for inspection by the government. But the government scarcely intervened, and never for political motives—for example in order to try to encourage labour, rather than capital-intensive, investment. Nationalisation caused no changes in management structure, except at the very top, and the Communist- controlled unions seemed equally concerned to prevent any diminution in the efficiency with which Setenave had been run under private control. Management consulted once a week with a workers' committee, composed of non-union officials democratically elected from the shop floor, but in general such consultation had constructive results. The workers in Setenave actually came up with their own idea of an extra night shift to overcome the loss of production that resulted from power cuts during the dry summer of 1975. The workers' commit- tee was generally concerned with issues affecting the workforce, and, although general investment and policy were discussed, the committee never sought to dictate company decisions in advance.

But efficient management was not enough without a wider economic recovery. Some of the investments the state had taken on were large and long-term in the extreme. The biggest of these was the Sines complex in southern Portugal, an attempt to build a huge petro-chemical, steel and mining centre and a new port in an area of high unemployment and little development. Sines was projected to cost a total of over $3 billion by 1985, when it would start yielding real returns. But the hike in oil prices had made the petrochemical side of it economically dubious. And although none of Portugal's successive governments, especially not Soares's, could really spare the money to go on building, the country was too deeply committed to the project. Too much had already been spent to be written off. Too many workers—7000—were employed on the project to lay them off. The hope was to finish it and reap whatever reward there was as quickly as possible.

The problem with the smaller companies that the state had taken over was that most of them were money losers, either because of what happened to them during the brief period when they were managed exclusively by the workers, or because they had been rescued by the state from bankruptcy at the insistence of the workers in the first place. So the public sector had a feeble base from which to launch an industrial recovery. And as proposed increases in taxes were insuffi-cient to cover even the increased cost of existing public services, more and more of the money going to the public sector came directly from credit that should have been available, from the nationalised banks, to the private sector. The private sector still accounted for nine-tenths of Portugal's exports, and about three-quarters of its employment. As many as half of those employed by the private sector worked for small firms of under ten people, and in the interior of Portugal pay and productivity were low. But because of its export orientation, and because the private sector was concentrated in areas—such as textiles and canned food production—where Portuguese goods were still competitive in international markets, the only real chances of an investment revival seemed to lie in private-sector investment.

The political impossibility of convincing large sectors of the Socialist party of these arguments led Soares into a growing rift with President Eanes. Soares, as always, was acting on the principle that he could only carry his own supporters with him when events had done the persuading for him; and the army's growing impatience was itself a useful stick with which to beat his supporters. Eanes's first intervention took place shortly before Soares's September speech, after he had been warned by the vigorous governor of the bank of Portugal, Silva Lopes,

E

that a first draft of the speech was too woolly both in analysis and proposals to carry any sort of conviction abroad. The analysis was hardened—Soares attacked absenteeism and political strikes, he pointed to a decline of 35–40 per cent in Portuguese industrial production—but his threats of wages and prices controls were still vague. As the year moved on, Soares seemed to have only one, uncontroversial weapon—import taxes, which were largely aimed against luxuries; petrol was taxed to more than $3 a gallon; VAT of up to 20 per cent was imposed on luxuries; an import surcharge of between 30 per cent and 60 per cent was introduced; and eventually an imports deposit scheme was passed. But the underlying structural problems of the economy remained.

Within his own party, though, Soares was far from idle. He elevated the able minister of commerce and tourism, Antonio Barreto, who favoured getting private investment off the ground again, to the job of minister of agriculture, when the left-winger Lopes Cardoso was fired in November. Barreto collected the additional post of minister of industry in January 1977 when Walter Rosa, his predecessor, resigned after a family scandal. Soares's main target during his first six months in office was a restoration of peace in the agricultural sector. Food imports were now adding a $450 million burden to Portugal's balance of payments, after being almost in surplus in 1973. About 52 per cent of Portugal's food came from abroad by the second half of 1976, as a result first of the explosion in domestic demand, and second of the slump in agricultural production.

Agricultural production had fallen for several reasons. First the government continued an old Salazarist policy of deliberately paying farmers low prices for their products in order to keep down politically sensitive food prices. Second, because of the mismanagement and demoralisation induced among farmers by the agricultural seizures of 1975, Soares's reappointment of Lopes Cardoso as minister of agriculture in July 1975 was a near disaster. Cardoso was an old-fashioned Socialist idealist who believed in the expropriation of all agricultural land in Portugal. After the northern farmers' uprising in the summer of 1975, he reluctantly accepted that his party could scarcely go ahead and urge the takeover of all the smallholdings there. But he stuck to his conviction about the larger estates of the centre and the south. The total expropriated so far, 1½ million acres, was not enough. At least 1 million acres more should go. After that, the government should start seeing to the grievances of small farmers who claimed that they had been illegally expropriated during the revolution. The ministry of agriculture, in addition, had become like an open well of money for the regional institutes of agrarian reform, many of which were controlled by Communists, and for the farm co-operatives.

Mario Soares knew he was sitting on a powder keg over land reform. The farmers were still prepared to use militancy—a food blockade on Lisbon—to secure their aims. President Eanes was also insistent on the need to give back land illegally taken over. Carefully selecting, with Antonio Barreto's advice, a token number—101—of farms expropriated under particularly unjustifiable circumstances, he insisted that Lopes Cardoso hand the land back to its former owners. Cardoso argued that the land restored should not come from land already taken over, but land eligible for expropriation in the future: sitting agricultural co-operatives should not be displaced. But Soares was adamant, and in October, in some cases accompanied by police, some of the former owners came back into their own. Others, more timidly, accepted uncashable government bonds in lieu of their old properties. The bold ones soon found themselves beset by problems, as the hostile co-operatives around them tried to deny them essential farm services and blacked them from agricultural markets.

But at the Socialist party congress held in November, Lopes Cardoso lent tacit support to an attempt to put up a rival slate of candidates for the party's central committee. The slate won one-fifth of the seats, and Soares, always swift in retribution where his personal power inside the party was concerned, took the opportunity to fire Cardoso. The fallen minister retired to the modest comforts of his small apartment in a working-class district of Lisbon, to act as a nucleus for potential left-wing opposition to Soares within the party. 'I and Mario Soares don't disagree about the end of a Socialist society. We just disagree about the speed of getting there,' he told the author.

The new minister, Antonio Barreto, moved quickly to control the flow of credit pouring unabated into the agricultural co-operatives. He cut off credit altogether to the worst offenders, giving them a time-limit to get their accounting in order. He charged civil servants in his own ministry with perpetuating frauds to help the co-operatives. He prepared plans to return reservas—plots of less than seventy-five acres or, under an accounting system, worth up to 50,000 points—which every expropriated owner who had previously lived on his land could claim back. He proposed alterations to the Goncalves law governing agricultural tenants, which had incensed the northern smallholders. He parcelled out land to be returned on adjoining plots so that owners could guard against intimidation by the surrounding co-operatives. And he started discussions with the Portuguese farmers' union, CAP, on how to encourage northern farmers voluntarily to join collectives such as the one that already existed in the northern region of Famalicao, for the marketing and production of crops like wine and barley. As one of the farmers' most militant leaders put it, reasonably:

Of course we accept that the present system of small holdings is grossly inefficient. Most farmers here grow cereal crops, although cereal-growing is only efficient in the large estates of the south. If we enter the Common Market, our products will be exposed to strong competition, and we must be in a position to face it.

Vitor Constancio, who led the economic team in Portugal's negotiations for membership of the EEC, gave a blunt warning.

There are far too many people on the land in Portugal. If we are ever to be competitive, there must be a reduction in the agricultural labour force. And that will entail an industrial revival to absorb the surplus labour from the country.

But the size of the agricultural challenge was underlined in April 1977 when Barreto claimed that the policies of the often dictatorially run co-operatives (critics of the Communists were expelled from them) would cause a 80 per cent drop in the wheat and barley crop, and a 30 per cent drop in oats. Two years of slumping agricultural investment, of surplus labour, of mismanaged land use, of ploughing barren soil and of slaughtering breeding stock for food had taken their toll.

Soares's second attack was on the labour front. By late 1976 he had become convinced of the need for wage restraint, and this was in fact introduced in March 1977 as a 15 per cent limit. To enforce his authority against a Communist-led Intersindical, he launched a frontal attack on its hold over the workers. Here he was ill-served by the minister of labour, Marcelo Curto, who was thought to be left-wing but whose flamboyant life-style quickly cost him the support of the pro-Communist unions. Soares and Curto first encouraged unions to join the Socialist umbrella organisation, 'Carta Aberta', named after an 'open letter' to the press some Socialist unions had sent in 1975 to protest against Communist domination of Intersindical. About eighty of Portugal's 340 unions joined Carta Aberta. Next, they cut off the subsidies that employers had to pay towards Intersindical by law, a relic from the days when the unions were a tame part of Salazar's corporate state. But shop stewards began collecting the dues from union members during working hours, disrupting proceedings and compelling employees to pay up for a peaceful life, so the move backfired.

Intersindical leaders also hit back at the Socialist tactics by holding a 'Congress of All Trades Unions', to which the Socialists were invited to send a token delegation, which Curto angrily refused to do, claiming that the April elections had proved that the Socialists commanded more rank-and-file support than the Communists. The Socialist party was itself split on the issue, and Soares slung out of the party in January a group of activists, including two deputies, for advocating that Carta Aberta join forces with Intersindical. Another Socialist union leader, Kalidas Barreto, attended the Congress of All Trades Unions hoping for a dialogue between the two parties. But his membership of the Socialist party lasted only until April. Curto himself was fired the same month for his lack of results. Broadly, though, Soares seemed to be winning the main point: despite a number of clarion calls to strike by a tactically edgy Communist party, the 15 per cent limit on wage claims seemed to hold.

Soares moved more slowly still in other areas where he was trying to sort out the economic tangle left after the revolution. He promised a revision of the foreign investment code, originally introduced by Admiral Pinheiro de Azevedo, which limited the repatriation of profits, but this only materialised in the summer of 1977. Soares proposed to pull the state out of 200 money-losing small firms, but took his time doing so. He proposed to regulate the workers' committees that had sprung up in industry, but was soon bogged down in the controversy this generated from both sides: on the one hand, Intersindical demanded prior vetting of management policy and investment decisions, and on the other leading industrialists like Antonio Barreto, managing director of Lisnave, said bluntly that they would not go on working under a system of prior consultation: 'Modern management requires fast decisions. I am prepared to consult the workers after my decisions, as I already do my shareholders, but not before.' Soares tried to limit absenteeism, which was dropping anyway, by passing a law giving employers wide-ranging powers to dismiss workers for a variety of sins. In practice, few employers were willing to risk the industrial disputes that might follow a strict enforcement of this law.

Soares proposed another law giving guarantees that no more private industry could be nationalised, but he moved slowly on compensation for the former owners of industries already nationalised. Antonio Vasco de Mello, the able, crotchety head of Portugal's chief private employers federation, the Confederation of Portuguese Industry (CIP) argued strongly that the state should allow some form of private banking in competition with the state; even in France, he pointed out, private banks existed just to keep the near-monopoly state sector on its toes. And Portugal's banking system lacked specialisation in credit management, was hidebound by bureaucratic procedures, and was still labouring under the suspicions of businessmen whose accounts had been examined and sometimes made public when bank clerks took them over briefly in 1975.

Despite the gradual stabilisation of economic policy, a private investment revival was slow, largely because of continuing uncertainty over the Socialist government's intention and political future (although few bankers can have feared that the far-left had any prospect of winning power: Portugal had nowhere to go but right). Portugal also desperately needed foreign money to tide its balance of payments over the period of economic adjustment, but countries were reluctant to lend to a country showing scant signs of economic recovery. In the end it was America which gave Portugal $300 million in credits in February, and America and West Germany who put together a further $700 million in June, that kept the country on the rails. Portugal hoped for at least another $1 billion over the following year, as renewed remittances of foreign exchange and tourist earnings provided proof that the worst for Portugal's balance of payments was over. But would the right-wing colonels' political impatience break before Soares began to reap the fruits of his gradualist economic policies?

*   *   *

For two years the struggle between right and left, between civilians and the army, between different personalities and all shades of political coloration, between economic and political interest groups had been raging on at the expense of proper government. Portugal's rushed withdrawal from its former colonies and the destruction of the country's already distorted economic system had laid up enormous political and social problems for her which had been all but ignored in the struggle for political power. The politicking and personality struggles, as became sadly apparent, did not disappear after Soares's government was sworn in, although President Eanes had removed one of the most explosive ingredients in the mixture by bottling up the army.

But events for the first time began to dictate politics. Portugal's social and economic problems had caught up with the politicians. The Socialist government's fate, General Eanes's fate, the fate of democracy itself, would be decided not by the subtlety of party or army political manoeuvring, or by trials of strength between small numbers of armed men. It would be decided by the government's ability to navigate through Portugal's economic and social maelstrom. The MFA had opened the Pandora's box back in 1974. It seemed all too clear that unless Mario Soares and the other civilian politicians could get the situation under control, the army would step in to do the job, and possibly restore Portugal to the museum of Europe whence it had escaped.

Nobody knows exactly how many refugees from Angola reached Portugal during the winter of 1975/76. About $\frac{1}{2}$ million registered, and about $\frac{1}{2}$ million more were thought to have come with them. The total of 1 million was more than the number of Algerian refugees that came to France in the 1960s, and in proportion to the population of the country, six times greater. In France the Algerian refugees have been a force for political instability and social discontent that has not yet been fully dampened. In Portugal both threats were more acute still.

Most of the refugees came in the daily airlift from Luanda, the capital of Angola. Others escaped in rickety boats from areas where the fighting had cut them off from reaching the Angolan capital. Many drowned in the treacherous waters of the Bay of Benguela. The air-lifted refugees could only take a handful of possessions, and the Angolan money they brought proved to be worthless, as Lisbon banks refused to exchange it. Most of the refugees had come originally from impove-rished peasant families in northern Portugal, or had worked on the farms of southern Portugal. In Angola they had gone into the admini-strative or trading jobs that were theirs for the taking in a colonial society. Fully two-thirds of the returning refugees worked in service industries while only 20 per cent were industrial workers, and only 4 per cent worked as farmers. Many of them grew relatively rich, employed black Angolan servants, and had large families: half the refugees—or *retornados*—were under sixteen.

On reaching Lisbon, some of them made their way as best they could to the houses of their poor relatives in the country, to try to begin anew what they had run away from years earlier. The majority, though, had nowhere to live and were herded into refugee camps on the outskirts of Lisbon. Others built rough shacks there out of hard-board, old crates, dustbins, corrugated iron, anything that came to hand. The camps were overcrowded, but government fears about the political uses to which hungry refugees could be put ensured that they had enough food, and that there were enough doctors and medical facilities to prevent any serious epidemics from breaking out.

Pinheiro de Azevedo's government set up the institute for Aid to National Refugees, IARN, to administer help to the retornados in 1976. IARN had a budget of $308 million in 1976, over one-third of which went on housing, the rest on medicines, clothes and schools. Refugees were paid an allowance of $26 a month per single person, $52 for married couples, $6 for each child under age, and $6 more for each child over eighteen. The allowances were in fact higher than the social pension being paid to ordinary unemployed Portuguese, which was only $13 a month in urban areas and $7 a month in country areas. From an early stage both Pinheiro's and Soares's governments tried to dilute the problem by getting the refugees into jobs as quickly as possible. IARN's head, Lieutenant-Colonel Goncalves Ribeiro, drew up a plan setting aside $170 million to help the refugees set up their own businesses, although the scheme has cost a colossal $4820 for each new job provided, usually at the expense of Portuguese peasants on small farms. By the end of 1976, only 33,000 refugees had been found jobs of any kind, and over 100,000 of the refugees registered with IARN were still looking for work. The real figure was probably more than twice as many.

The subsidies being ladled out to the refugees were one source of friction between the two Portuguese communities. The retornados brought with them *liambra*, their own form of marijuana, as well as hard drugs, which began to spread through a previously drug-free Lisbon. Impoverished refugee families set their teenage daughters to walk the central areas of Lisbon as cut-price prostitutes, angering the residents. Crime, always low in Portugal, began to multiply: settlers robbed taxi drivers of their fares, and in a few well-publicised cases, killed them as well. The number of murders in Portugal in 1975 doubled to forty-three. When space for the refugees ran out in the camps, the government took to commandeering hotels, pensions and holiday accommodation, giving cut-price payments to their proprietors. This was accepted by the proprietors during the winter, but strongly resented when the tourist season came round. Luxury hotels in Lisbon were overrun by gangs of refugee children, riding up and down in the lifts and putting them out of order, and breaking the furniture and fittings.

The *ad hoc* and chaotic nature of IARN's administration in the early days soon gave rise to abuses in the administration of welfare payments. Rich Angolans started claiming the payments, and refugees billeted to receive IARN housing subsidies claimed payments by giving the addresses of their hotels without revealing that they were hotels. The worst abuses came from the Portuguese side, as owners of lodging houses crammed tens of Angolans into one room and then claimed payment for lodging each of them separately. The retornados were finally ejected from first class hotels in the summer of 1976, and from all hotels in the spring of 1977.

Considering the strains, it was surprising how little violence broke out between the two communities. There were demonstrations outside Portuguese banks refusing to lend the retornados money in the winter of 1975, but most passed off peacefully. The party that cultivated closest links with the Angolans was the Centre Democratic party, which did much to pour oil on the troubled waters. The MDLP had its own links with the Angolans until it broke up on the autumn of 1975, but refugee leaders were keener on working for a return to Africa than a change of government in Portugal. Lieutenant-Colonel Santos e Castro, one of the MDLP's leaders, who worked for a time as chief of staff to Holden Roberto's National Front for the Liberation of Angola (see Chapter 11), recruited men in Lisbon to go out and fight against the Popular Movement's victory in the ex-colony. But refugee opinion, as expressed in their newspaper, *O Retornado*, was largely negative, expressing for example a violent hatred of Rosa Coutinho, the last Portuguese high commissioner in Angola, and of Vasco Goncalves. But it failed to channel itself into insurrectionary activity in Portugal. The retornados tried to run their own candidate, Pompilio da Cruz, in the 1976 presidential elections, but he was ruled out because his papers were not in order.

Not until March 1977 did a charismatic political leader emerge to command retornado support. The leader was General Galvao de Melo, who used his post as an independent Centre Democrat deputy to pester the government with awkward questions, asking whether Portuguese political prisioners remained in Angola and Mozambique. Galvao openly called for an inquiry into the decolonisation of Angola and Mozambique. He lambasted Rosa Coutinho and Vasco Goncalves, and for good measure attacked ex-president Costa Gomes himself. His playing to the gallery was a departure from the extreme caution he had previously displayed in Portuguese domestic politics, and helped to inspire a growing rift with Freitas do Amaral and the Centre Democratic leaders, whom he regarded as flirting too closely with the Socialist government.

In early April 1977 a near-riot took place outside the national assembly, as a large crowd of retornados battled with police to get into the building and listen to their champion's searching questions. The retornados were only calmed when Galvao de Melo came out to speak to them. President Eanes himself publicly admonished the reserve air force general for his demagoguery, but he was powerless to stop Galvao de Melo emerging as the leader of a new, highly political, refugee organisation. Later in April, Freitas do Amaral formally expelled him from the Centre Democratic party. Where the general would take his flock of 1 million remained an anxiety to all the democratic parties.

The refugee problem was complicated towards the end of 1976 by a new flow from Portuguese Timor, where a civil war still sputtered on, and from Mozambique, where expropriations and spells of imprisonment in Samora Machel's jails were scaring many of the 20,000 Portuguese settlers still remaining out of the country. A large number of those living in Mozambique when independence was granted had opted not to take Mozambique nationality, preferring the cardboard reassurance of retaining Portuguese nationality. These included not just the white Portuguese settlers, but many of the Asian and Chinese settlers who worked in the colony, as well as black civil servants and officials who feared that their service in the old colonial government might be a liability under Mozambique's new rulers. In March 1977, President Machel abruptly ordered the expulsion of those holding Portuguese passports, and the flow of refugees increased to about 100 a week. The deadline was later extended because the president was having second thoughts about expelling some of the country's few skilled administrators and technicians, but in the event few stayed behind.

The new refugees brought a colour problem with them, although, the number of coloured immigrants was probably small enough to prevent any outright spread of racialism, not a vice to which Portuguese are particularly prone anyway. They also posed a new challenge to the government's overstretched resources. The Portuguese wanted to keep the flow of refugees down to the minimum possible, and not to encourage a new exodus of Mozambiquans suffering from the increasing economic deprivations of living under the Frelimo government there. So the government decided to cut off welfare payments to any retornados coming after 30 November 1976, in order to lessen the attractions of escaping to Portugal. They tried, too, to cut down on the number of permits being issued in Mozambique, but, as one official in the Portuguese consulate there put it, 'What can you do? People come and say they will be thrown into one of Machel's camps for their services to our empire. You have to give them the visa.'

The welfare cut-off proved unworkable once the refugees had reached Lisbon. The Portuguese Red Cross took on the task of doing something to clothe, house and feed the refugees on their arrival. Understaffed, underequipped, working in cramped offices in the small Red Cross building in west Lisbon, the organisation conducted a running telephone battle with the government to get aid for the new arrivals. Retornados often had to wait whole days at Lisbon airport as Red Cross officials refused to move them until one ministry or another gave a guarantee that it would put up the money to keep them. 'Everything is done on an *ad hoc* basis, everything is a tug of war with the ministers,' complained Captain Carlos Godinho, a former Angolan officer working on one of the Red Cross sections, 'but you just can't leave these people on the tarmac.' Only in May did the government agree to give the new refugees the same benefits enjoyed by the Angolan refugees.

The Mozambiquan refugees were as politically active as the Angolan ones. An exiled anti-Communist black Mozambiquan leader, Domingos Arouca, set up his own liberation organisation, the United Democratic Front of Mozambique (FUMO) in Lisbon, where it recruited soldiers from the exile community and co-ordinated resistance operations in a large part of the Mozambiquan countryside. Arouca's main aim was to topple Frelimo, preferably with South African help, and allow the retornados to return to their country of adoption. His closest sympathies in Portugal lay with General Galvao de Melo, although he carefully kept his organisation from getting mixed up in

Portuguese internal politics. 'We have no illusions that a Portuguese government will ever send soldiers to fight in Africa again,' he acknowledged to the author realistically. In the likely event, though, that the retornados never find a home to return to in Africa, they are likely to be a political danger and a social burden for many years to come. 'There is no refugee problem,' Mario Soares said in March. 'By the end of 1980 the word retornado should have disappeared from the daily vocabulary,' echoed Lieutenant-Colonel Goncalves Ribeiro of IARN. They were counting their chickens before they were hatched.

The retornados contributed to the chronic unemployment that had come to beset post-revolutionary Portugal. The Salazar regime had claimed blandly that unemployment did not exist in Portugal. It did, but it was concealed or exported. Many Portuguese emigrated to Africa and to the booming industrial economies of Western Europe in the 1950s and 1960s because of the scarcity and low pay of the jobs at home. Large numbers of these European emigrants came back when labour outlets in Europe dried up in the 1974/75 recession. Many Portuguese under the old dictatorship had part-time jobs as boot-blacks, or as occasional farm labourers, or as domestic servants, or in some fringe government activity such as acting as one of the innumerable porters hanging around Lisbon's ministries, or selling lottery tickets, or weaving at home for the underpaid Portuguese textile industry. Underemployment was chronic, but by and large putting a few part-time jobs together provided a survivable minimum for most Portuguese poor families, although they lacked the most basic consumer goods.

Soaring wages in Portugal after the 1974 coup at first pumped money into the pockets of the people employed in these fringe jobs, as demand rose. Then higher wages forced firms, especially small ones, to go bankrupt and fire their employees. Workers belonging to the big unions or the industrially advanced sectors of the economy, near Lisbon and Setubal and Oporto and Braga, had both their earnings and employment protected. Industrial workers in these coastal areas were earning about $180 a month, way above the minimum wage of $115 a month introduced by the Socialist government, and the wages actually being paid to workers in country areas of as low as $50 a month by inefficient firms that could afford to pay no more.

The soaring cost of living—prices more than doubled over the 1975/77 period—outstripped the average rise in labour costs (about 80 per cent) and hit sharply at the living standards of low-paid industrial workers and the unemployed. Small peasant farm labourers living a marginal existence on the land were not too badly affected by the rise in consumer prices, but two-fifths of the newly unemployed were industrial workers. 'They are the people we are really concerned about,' labour minister Marcelo Curto told the author in February 1977. 'They are the people that could cause rioting on the streets.' By then unemployment was estimated at 750,000, fully a quarter of Portugal's 3 million workforce.

Both Pinheiro de Azevedo's Socialist-inclined government, and Soares's Socialist government tried to do something to cushion the hardest hit unemployed. They were starting from scratch. Beyond church charity and a rudimentary health service, government welfare services hardly existed in Salazar's Portugal. Pinheiro introduced a social pension, which Soares later increased to about $13 a month per person. But the social pension was only effectively available in the advanced coastal regions of Portugal. Retirement pensions, which were also only available to a fairly small number of people, were raised to about $20 a month.

The biggest initiatives were made in trying to modernise the health service. The minister of social affairs, Armando Bacelar, an elderly, vague, Socialist intellectual, introduced in early 1977 a scheme to provide medical care free to all those who could not afford it—peasants, the unemployed—and at low cost to the rest. He also offered financial incentives to encourage Portuguese doctors, of whom there was no shortage (1 for every 500 people by 1980) to practise medicine in the provinces. The minister hoped that lucrative private practices would die out in competition with the new state health scheme. But the fact was that too little had been earmarked from an already tight budget in 1977 to suggest that the state system would be able to set up the facilities to achieve Armando Bacelar's goals. If doctors began to be drawn into national health practice, it was because many of the old private patients had fled abroad or could not afford the fees any more.

*   *   *

One of the toughest men in Mario Soares's government turned out to be the minister of education, Sottomayor Cardia. It was a job that required a firm hand. By the time he took office, he faced chaos in the classrooms. The system was comprehensive in some areas, selective in others, perpetually disrupted by strikes and committee meetings, and was heavily politicised at the expense of its academic standards. The surprising thing about education in Portugal was that it was one of the few areas where the old regime actually turned out to be more enlightened than the new, where the 1974 coup did clear harm.

Under Salazar, the educational system was backward and politi- cised. History and geography were designed to educate Portuguese children about the importance in the world of the Portuguese empire. Textbooks impressed on children that the empire was as large as the whole of Western Europe. The schools system was also highly selective. Middle class children went to private schools (the most famous of which was run by Mario Soares's father). Education was compulsory in primary schools only until the age of twelve. After twelve most children left school and went to work; the rest went either to *lyceums*, which were largely concentrated in the country, and usually had a single teacher for all subjects, or to technical schools, largely concentrated in the towns, which, in the better ones, had different teachers for different subjects. Lyceum pupils could, after three years' education, try for a further two and then go to university. Promising technical school pupils were shunted mechanically along to technical institutes and then into industrial jobs. After the age of twelve it was almost impossible for bright, urban working-class pupils to get into university.

That cautious liberal Marcello Caetano was radical in one area alone. He appointed a rising intellectual star, Veiga Simao, to supervise educational reform in Portugal in 1973. Simao dispatched study teams to different European countries. He was a staunch believer in comprehensive education, and had been known to say that if he lived in Britain he would have supported the Labour party—quite an admission for a minister under a right-wing dictatorship. He was not popular with his conservative colleagues, and only under threat of resignation did he manage to get his educational reform through the cabinet in 1973. He was to be the only one of Caetano's ministers who retained for a time a government post under the MFA—as Portuguese ambassador to the United Nations.

If Simao survived for a time, his reforms did not. Under his plans all children would spend four years at primary level, where they would be taught by a single teacher in all subjects, much as under the old system. Between the ages of twelve and sixteen children would have different teachers for different subjects—but the technical and lyceum schools would be fully integrated into a comprehensive system. Only at sixteen would those children who stayed on at school get the option of going to university or technical colleges. Even students at technical colleges would get the chance to go and do advanced courses at university. Under a pilot scheme, a large number of children in areas where there was a shortage of teachers would be taught by television programmes. The 12–16-year-olds involved could thus be supervised by just one teacher, but could get the benefit of several different teachers on television.

Simao also planned to do away with the centralised and extremely rigid marking system, under which all work had to be graded on a scale of 0–20 marks. The new system would have been fully comprehensive and more advanced than that in most European countries. Simao planned to double the number of Portuguese universities—from the four at world-famous Coimbra, Oporto and Lisbon, where there were two—to eight. The four new ones were planned at Evora, Braga, Aveiro and Lisbon. The whole scheme would have been expensive, but in 1973 Simao was confident that the money would be available.

After the April 1974 coup, the schools and universities became a prime target for political activism. Successive ministers of education were faced by a proliferation of committees of management in the universities and the schools. The committees were headed by militant left-wing students, teachers, and workers in the schools. A series of strikes all but closed the universities through the autumn of 1974, as the committees struggled for control. Within the ministry of education itself, left-wing administrators purged their right-wing colleagues, and shipped aboard several hundred left-wing teachers, who replaced the political teachings of Salazar with those of Marx. The old centralised marking and examination system was abolished, and in many schools students were given the right to evaluate their own work, or were evaluated as a group. Simao's reforms were stopped, leaving the educational system as a British-style hybrid between the old system and a new comprehensive one. Many parents withdrew their children from the schools altogether for fear they would be politically indoctrinated, and schools were closed for long periods in many parts of the country.

It fell to Sottomayor Cardia, one of Soares's youngest, closest colleagues, to try to bring some order back into the system when he became minister of education in July 1976. This he did by firing 300 left-wingers from the ministry of education and restoring a centralised marking system. Cardia's attempts to do away with the management committees were challenged by sporadic strike action, but his determination prevailed. Political textbooks were for the first time in half a century expunged from Portugal's schools. Cardia's own views on schooling were strongly disciplinarian, but he considered an effective educational system to be the indispensable minimum for bringing Portugal up to date with modern Europe. For the moment, however, he lacked the funds to go ahead with Veiga Simao's reform programme.

*   *   *

For a visitor to Lisbon in April 1977, three years after the coup, Portugal's society presented a face largely unchanged since Salazar's day. The differences did not seem to run very deep. Lisbon's narrow, steep, picturesque streets were dirtier and pitted with holes. The walls were papered with political posters. Lisbon's street-sellers peddled political tracts and soft-core pornography openly, where neither were permitted before. Lisbon's cinemas were inundated with ten years' worth of sexual liberation from the European cinema. The newspapers, now freed from both Salazarist and Communist control, published a refreshing diversity of opinions, although many of the ones founded by Salazarist industrialists were now being run at a loss by the State.

The police were more inhibited and lax in their attitude towards traffic infringements, prostitution and petty crime than before April 1974; even so, where once they had been denounced as fascists for enforcing the most commonplace laws, they were now beginning to be respected again. Juridically, too, a paralysed legal system had begun to work and sentence offenders. Public administration was if anything less competent than before, as layers of administrators appointed by conflicting Portuguese governments over the three years did battle with one another. The largest and most welcome change was that the Portuguese had lost their fear of authority. The cowed, furtive, don't-want-to-know look that was all too common in Portugal's streets under Salazar had been replaced by a brusque self-confidence.

But the economic revolution had not come. Industry had been hurt, the country impoverished, some fortunes had been lost, but the working people had nothing to show for it. Cars were still predominantly old models. Young people had caught the European craze for cheap denims and jeans, but their elders still stuck to their old-fashioned suits and traditional dresses. Despite inflation and food shortages, many of Lisbon's restuarants remained underpriced and unchanged. So did the clattering buses, the slow, bare, trains, and the unobtainable taxis.

The lack of change was all the more evident in the countryside of the north, where the rural peasantry had been largely untouched, both in material wealth and working habits. Even in the south, the Alentejo's co-operatives had scarcely affected people's wealth and living standards. Anti-religious feeling had become widespread in the south—but then it always had been during periods of political freedom. Northerners continued to be devout churchgoers, as they always had been. Attitudes towards the family, towards women, towards sex, towards religion would no doubt evolve over the years—but the Portuguese, unlike the Spaniards, had not had years of economic growth and exposure to mass tourism to prepare themselves for change. Women in business, much less in politics, were still a rarity: doors were still opened for men first, women second.

The political upheaval and the disruption of the country's economy had not produced a social revolution; only economic prosperity would.

14 Colonels in the wings

The first six months of Mario Soares's government saw a lull in the fierce political and military in-fighting which had overshadowed Portuguese politics since the revolution. Only within the Socialist party, and between the Socialists and the Communists, did the struggle go on unabated. The problems facing the country divided a polyglot party that had only been united by its vacuous faith in a Socialism that Portugal had never experienced, and its resistance to the dictatorship that the Communists had attempted to reimpose on the Portuguese people. It was no suprise that the inexperienced administrators running the Socialist party opted for internal recrimination rather than positive solutions. But it was certainly dangerous for Portugal's democracy.

The Communist party's attitudes were meant to be dangerous. The party had been under serious strains most of the year. Many of the party's opponents considered that its primary objectives had been to see that Portuguese Africa was handed over to Marxist liberation movements, and that it had never entertained any real hopes in Portugal itself. This was an exaggeration. Throughout the summer of 1975, Alvaro Cunhal doggedly believed that the revolution could triumph in Portugal. He had an intense, primitive, Marxist-Leninist faith in the need to spread the party through positions of power and influence as rapidly as possible; and he had only contempt for power gained through the ballot box. The election results in 1975 and 1976 were not, for him, reversals; he had not expected to do much better.

But he had hoped that his friends in the army—Vasco Goncalves, Costa Martins, Varela Gomes, Ramiro Correia—would have more influence, and that the Marxism of people like Otelo would not be as lightheaded. Cunhal could be well satisfied with what the radical soldiers had achieved in Portuguese Africa. He was well satisfied with what the Communists had gained in the unions and the industrial belt round Lisbon and Setubal. He was well satisfied with control of a geographic area which covered about one-third of the country. His reverses were disappointing, but he was not going to change the tactics which had achieved such success in so many fields.

Many of his colleagues in the party's central committee considered his tactics too intransigent. Almost to a man they accepted his tactical opportunism—there were no democrats in the party leadership, which set it apart from the Spanish and Italian parties. All of them preferred the revolutionary path to power. But, frustrated in that direction, some of them turned their eyes to the growing success of 'Euro-communism' in Italy and France. In Portugal too, they argued, the potential existed for becoming the major working class party by appearing to respect at least the norms of democracy. The case of Cunhal's critics became particularly strong when Mario Soares indicated that the Socialists would try to take office alone. The Communists could present themselves as the sole major alternative on the left at a time when the government would have to take extremely unpopular economic measures, which would impinge especially on the working classes. The chances were that Portuguese democracy would survive until the next election in 1978, and that the Socialist party's support among industrial workers would all but evaporate.

Support for this line crystallised around the party's parliamentary leader, Octavio Pato. Pato is a personally warmer, less intellectual man than Cunhal, with much of the appeal of a Eurocommunist politician. His main ally in the attempt to replace Cunhal was Aboim Ingles, who returned in the autumn of 1975 from Moscow. Ingles had the backing of the Russians, and was thought to supervise the money and logistical support that the Russian Communist party had been feeding to its Portuguese comrades. Ingles faithfully reflected the then view of the Russian party secretary, Leonid Brezhnev, that on balance the Euro-communists would do more good in Western Europe than harm. Brezhnev felt there was nothing wrong in a controlled experiment in Eurocommunism by a previously loyal pro-Russian party, as in France or Portugal, although he viewed the much more radical Italian and Spanish experiments with greater misgivings. As a temporary expedient to gain revolutionary power, eschewing revolutionary for democratic methods was fine.

Accordingly, Ingles had argued that Pato should stand as a Communist candidate for the presidency in 1975, as a test of his potential electoral attractions, although few people expected the Communists to put up a candidate at all. In this way the Russians could show that they were not being disloyal to their faithful old work-horse Cunhal, but could, if Pato succeeded, hint that it was time for the party's fiery prophet to gracefully make way for a more modern approach.

Pato had failed dismally, polling just 7 per cent of the vote, under half the normal Communist vote in general elections. Cunhal had been particularly shrewd in letting Pato go ahead and hang himself: his candidacy had taken place in the trough of the Communists' recent unpopularity. Pato was challenged on the left by the far better-known and more appealing figure of Otelo de Carvalho, and Communist supporters were understandably indifferent to their shadowy deputy

leader. Paradoxically, although Cunhal's hard-line image had made
him a multitude of enemies, it had made him the object of something
like adulation among his bedrock followers. The Communists' 14–18
per cent constituency liked Cunhal's toughness better than Pato's
modernism. Cunhal had become synonymous with Portuguese
Communism in their eyes.

Cunhal's leadership was from that moment beyond question. But
the debate about tactics simmered on. It became clear through the
first six months of Socialist government that the right's strength in the
army was growing by the day, and that the only alternative to the
democratic experiment was a right-wing coup. If the Communists
went on frustrating Portugal's economic recovery, if the Socialist
government failed abjectly to control events, it could only be a matter
of time before the colonels moved in. Cunhal himself was loath to see the
power still held by his party being banished altogether under another
military dictatorship of the right. At the same time, though, certain
elements in the Russian embassy in Lisbon were pressing him that in
fact that would be the best solution. The hardest line coming from
Moscow at the time was aiming for two objectives: the relatively mild
one of stopping Portugal joining the Common Market and the more
important one of preventing Spain from becoming a democracy, and
joining the Common Market, or, worse, joining NATO and becoming
a bulwark for the alliance in the western Mediterranean. Both objectives would be hampered by a right-wing military coup in Lisbon. The
Common Market would instantly reject Portugal's application to join.
And the powerful Spanish lobby, particularly in the army, that argued
that Iberia and its ex-colonies were inherently incapable of democracy
(fourteen out of the nineteen Spanish- and Portuguese-speaking
colonies in Latin America were military dictatorships) would be
reinforced. Spain's democratic experiment would be made to seem
an aberration in the peninsula's history, not the natural evolution
of a nation grown mature enough to join the ranks of European
democracies.

Cunhal steered a middle course between the two groups. With
Aboim Ingles's support he was able to override the more impatient
Russian voices. At the same time, he decided to exert the party's
industrial strength against the Socialist government. A Communist
shop steward argued: 'We hate Soares, we hate Eanes; but they are
our only hope of avoiding a military coup. So the workers must be
patient for a time.' But the party still wanted to give the workers
leadership, even in the act of restraint. So what followed was a curious,
two-pronged Communist tactic of keeping up the strongest possible
vitriol against the Socialists, of threatening and holding strikes in non-
essential sectors, of resisting every attempt to diminish Communist

power in the Alentejo region, in the press and elsewhere—but never bringing events to a head. Strikes took place, but the Communist-controlled unions at the Lisnave and Setenave shipyards, where good foreign currency was being earned, stayed silent and wholly co-operative. Communist language was wildly intemperate, Communist actions were not. The only serious clashes occurred when the government began returning some of the land illegally expropriated in 1974 by the Communists to its former owners (see Chapter 13). Alvaro Cunhal's fear was that unless the Communist party put up a good show of defending the interests of the urban working classes, disaffected Socialists would move over to supporting a rejuvenated far-left group, possibly led by the still youthful Otelo.

The need for restraint was understood by the two right-wing parties. Neither wanted to be held responsible for renewed political instability in Portugal, which might lead to the return of soldiers impatient at the squabbles of civilians. For six months, both parties were on their best behaviour, voting for Socialist measures whenever they could, appeasing where they could, always steering clear of out-right condemnation of the government. These tactics were hard on the Centre Democratic leadership: the party's rank and file was militantly anti-Socialist. The maverick CDS deputy, General Galvao de Melo, indicated at an early stage that he did not favour letting the arrange-ment go on too long, although he steered well clear of any outright condemnation of his leader, Freitas do Amaral. Instead, he veered his attack towards the party's deputy leader, Amaro da Costa, who was friendly with Socialist parliamentary leaders, and had been known to support a coalition between the two parties. Sustained attacks on 'Adelinismo' made the jovial engineer's position tricky over the succeeding months, although he had Freitas do Amaral's full support.

Exactly the reverse conditions prevailed in the Social Democratic party (the Popular Democrats changed their name to Social Democrats in October 1976). Sa Carneiro and Magalhaes Mota were more impatient than their rank and file, some of whom, like Rebelo da Sousa, were in almost open rebellion. Sa Carneiro seemed eager to get his hands on power, and was longing to assert himself against the government. Unlike other party leaders, however, he was tired of the political game, and wanted soon to retire from the party; he just wanted to cut through the continuing mess, do what was right for Portugal, and then disappear as quickly as he could. He thought he saw better than anyone the speed with which events must move towards the right to forestall a new right-wing army coup. Frustrated in all his efforts to force Mario Soares into a coalition, frowned on by President Eanes, Sa Carneiro elapsed into a graceless tolerance of the

Socialist government's first six months in office. But as the Socialists frittered away those months of grace, the Social Democratic leader resolved to attack openly by the early new year. In January he visited Spain, and declared that Portugal was 'on the brink of bankruptcy'. This aroused a storm of protest from the Socialists who said he had no right to criticise his own country from abroad. In January, when Medina Carreira's woolly, large-scale spending budget was published, he resolved to vote against it.

This gave Freitas do Amaral his opportunity. Long aware of the ties between Eanes and the Socialist party, long convinced that Sa Carneiro couldn't blandly set aside the consideration that the Socialists were the country's largest party, the Centre Democratic leader decided to play the statesman. Freitas do Amaral had himself reached something of a crossroads in political life. Still only thirty-five, he was tired by the political infighting of the previous three years, and he wanted time to rest and reflect. The local election results were an acute political disappointment, and he returned to his secluded and luxurious house in a pinewood near Cascais to ponder whether he would stay leader of a party that had apparently peaked at 16 per cent. His uncompromising conservatism, at a time when conservatism was under fierce political attack in 1975, had won him, he knew, the respect of the increasingly restless right-wing soldiers. His uncompromising belief in democracy had earned him the respect of all the parties to his left. Increasingly he felt that his role was that of an above-the-battle, non-party figure, a man to whose consistency the country could turn in times of grave crisis. He held an underlyingly pessimistic view of democracy's chances for survival in Portugal, and at times seemed to yearn for a right-wing coup from which he could disassociate himself, go into exile, and return eventually, as Karamanlis did in Greece, to lead the country to prosperity and democracy. He had come to behave as a man much older than his years, a man whose virtuous private life was a model for the lifestyle of a modern European statesman. Freitas do Amaral was the natural leader of a country, not of a party with under one-fifth of the vote.

So, with Amaro da Costa's agile political mind working beside him, he used his party mercilessly. He forced it to abstain in the debate about the budget, and the Socialist government survived. At a stroke he earned the gratitude of the president, while insisting that his move was not made from support for government policy, but because he believed in democracy. 'Democracy is too fragile,' he told the author, 'to bring down a government after only six months in office, and in which the electorate has just reaffirmed its support [in the local elections].' His reputation for integrity was preserved—at the cost of alienating much support within the party.

But the party could not survive without Freitas do Amaral and his public appeal, and it knew it. In February, as rank and file disillusion grew against the critical unofficial deal with the Socialists, he met the party's regional leaders in Oporto, told them he would resign and asked them to fix the date and manner of his going. Every area leader pleaded with him to stay. At the next session he repeated his intention of going, and the area leaders pleaded once more. At the end of this meeting he said he would leave the decision to his wife—and she told him to stay. The truth was that he had been perfectly prepared to go if the direction in which he was leading the party had been called into question. By re-emphasising their dependence on him, the party leaders had given him *carte blanche* to do as he liked. The following April, Freitas do Amaral used his absolute powers to expel General Galvao de Melo, his long-standing rival, for criticising his leadership, for voicing vague aspirations for a return to right-wing dictatorship, and for championing the increasingly militant dissent of the retornados.

The same month, the Centre Democratic leader received his reward for acting responsibly: he was offered the post of chairman of a powerful administrative reform commission by President Eanes. Both Eanes and Freitas do Amaral agreed, however, that they would not go on supporting the government indefinitely: if the balance of payments failed to turn around by autumn, a new government should be given a try.

The decision to appoint Freitas do Amaral as chairman of the administrative reform commission was contested by Soares, who tried to restrict the terms of reference of the new body. The danger he and his closest strategist, the minister of social communication, Manuel Alegre, feared was that the president would grow to depend on Freitas do Amaral's constitutional advice. Not only was a coalition being created by stealth, but a kind of surrogate prime minister as well, taking decisions on matters of day-to-day administration. In April Soares appointed Alegre as his *chef de cabinet*, although all agreed he had been a disaster at the ministry. But he acted as a useful go-between with the president. Negotiations between Soares and Alegre and the president and his sharp young *chef de cabinet*, Henrique Granadeiro, dragged on into the summer.

But Soares knew that time was running out. The long-promised economic recovery showed little sign of arriving. America's president, Jimmy Carter, who in April had undertaken to try to persuade his fellow members of the IMF to provide a $1,500 million loan to tide Portugal over the year, only came up with $700 million in a joint American–German credit in June. Eanes was himself coming round to the view that loans were not only insufficient to help Portugal, but were positively harmful, simply buying time at the cost of adding to the burden of Portugal's balance of payments deficit. Eanes regarded the appointment of Freitas do Amaral as the minimum necessary to try to inject some backbone into the government, and to stave off the mutters of the militant colonels on his right.

Early in February, the two senior men at Eanes's elbow, Colonels Soares Carneiro and Jaime Neves, began again to meet on a regular basis as the 'operational FMU group'. In his contacts with both of them, Sa Carneiro forcefully made the point that they should seek to force the Socialists into a coalition with the Social Democrats. Both colonels strongly favoured the idea, and made their views known to the president. Early in February, Colonel Soares Carneiro also sought a meeting with Freitas do Amaral, at which he implied that the Centre Democratic leader was the politician most respected in the army, but was inexplicably supporting the Socialist government. Freitas do Amaral patiently tried to justify his position and his commitment to democracy, an exercise he was to repeat on 22 February 1977, when he met, for the first time, Jaime Neves, at the soldier's request. The appointment of Freitas do Amaral partially assuaged the colonels, and both of them decided to wait and see if anything would change by the autumn.

Sa Carneiro was confident, despite the temporary setback which his hopes for a coalition had suffered when Freitas do Amaral helped out the Socialists, that the colonels would bring things to a head in the autumn. Eanes himself had privately resolved to act by then to pre-empt them. He favoured a forced coalition or a government of technocrats only in the last resort. He strongly opposed Soares Carneiro's idea of a Gaullist-style presidential party which could win a general election and provide a convenient vehicle for direct presidential rule. Soares's slow slide to the right continued, as he suspended left-wing deputies like Lopes Cardoso and Kalidas Barreto in May. But it was beginning to be too slow to save him from a change of government in the autumn.

At the time of completing this book, Portugal seemed to be moving slowly away from the parliamentary system it had experienced for little more than a year. Much of the blame for this rests with the Socialist government, which failed to take the economic measures made urgent by the profligacy of the left-wing experiment in 1975. But, disturbing as the trend to the far right was becoming, Portuguese democracy had grown some extremely strong roots in the struggle against dictatorship. These included the solid support for democracy among voters; the strong desire for a European *raison d'être* after the African connection had been severed—and membership of the Common Market, like the claim to be a modern European society, is limited to democracies; and the tenacity of the democratic parties.

Further, Portugal's constitution allows a considerable give before democracy can be said to have been broken.

General Eanes does have the popular legitimacy of having won the support of more than three-fifths of the voters, and the constitution allows him considerable discretionary powers which he has not yet exercised. He can appoint any government which can command a majority in parliament; he can even, in the last resort, declare a state of emergency and govern by decree. Because General Eanes is so flatly committed to democracy, the colonels would in the last resort have to remove him from office to create a genuinely dictatorial system. And removing a popularly elected president who was also the Portuguese army's most effective recent commander will be no easy task. Portugal's democracy has the buffer of a strong president, and a strong presidential system. Freedom will not be relinquished without a struggle. The infant democracy in Portugal is a sturdy, healthy child, struggling in bleak conditions that would have killed a weaker baby.

*   *   *

Mario Soares's single-party government staggered on until December. Gradually the reluctance of the other parties to topple it, which had kept it in power, tapered into downright hostility. On 2 August, Alvaro Cunhal was the first to urge an immediate end to the government, and speedy elections. In October, the Social Democrats said they had had enough, and insisted they be included in the government. The Centre Democrats, miffed because Soares had stalled over Freitas do Amaral's appointment to head the administrative reform commission, announced that they too would be prepared to vote against the government in a vote of confidence.

The economy was going from worse to even worse. A new set of emergency measures was issued in August, which would allow the escudo to float downwards by 1 per cent a month. This was yet another bid to boost exports and curb imports. Interest rates were raised by more than 4 per cent, while taxes on consumer goods were raised by a further 8 per cent, and personal taxes went up, again. But the measures made scarcely a dent in the country's balance of payments deficit, which was running at about $1·2 billion—higher than the year before. The government's only real success was to secure observance of the 15 per cent wage increase ceiling—but inflation was fuelled by higher import prices and taxes still hovered around 30 per cent. Private investment and private industrial activity refused to pick up, as a consequence of the government's continued channelling of funds to the sluggish public sector.

The government's refusal to share power, coupled with the deepening economic crisis, aroused intense speculation in the autumn about whether President Eanes would intervene to resolve the impasse. But on 16 October, strict constitutionalist as he was, President Eanes refused once again to intervene openly. He asked instead for an understanding between government and opposition on an economic programme—of a kind that had been signed the month before between government and opposition parties in Spain. He also indirectly criticised the Social Democrats, making a reference to 'the sterile intransigence of permanent opposition'. Sa Carneiro bitterly concluded that the president had nailed his colours to the Socialist mast. From then on the Social Democratic leader began to wage a campaign of fierce criticism against the president for evading his responsibilities and for his alleged closeness to left-wing members of the council of revolution. The president's defenders argued that he was only making clear his distaste for any interference in the parliamentary process, which he feared might be used as an example by other officers who lacked the democratic base that he possessed.

Solidarity within the Socialist party itself was crumbling. The widely respected foreign minister, Jose Medeiros Ferreira, resigned early in October. Lopes Cardoso, the former agriculture minister, left the party at about the same time to found his own new faction on the left. The government was given a few more weeks of life when, on 11 November, Sa Carneiro resigned as leader of his party, in disagreement with his lieutenants, who were having second thoughts about his policy of total intransigence. Sa Carneiro was confident he would be re-elected as leader at a party assembly to be held in January, although he was to be proved wrong. But when Soares sought to take advantage of the split in the main opposition party by calling a vote of confidence for early December, to give his government the necessary credibility to negotiate a $50m IMF credit which would unlock a medium-term loan of $750m, the Social Democrats closed ranks. After a frenzied fortnight of negotiation, during which Soares canvassed support from the Social Democrats, the Centre Democrats and the Communists, his government was defeated by 159 votes to 100.

The spectre of new elections presented itself as Soares appeared to stand by his refusal to share power with any other party. All the parties were reluctant to force Portuguese voters to go to the polls for the fifth time in three years, because they feared that the Parliamentary deadlock would be recreated, that the Portuguese would abstain in large numbers, and that the army might be increasingly tempted to intervene. There seemed to be no middle way between Soares's rejection of a coalition and the conservative parties' demand for one. Soares's first inclination was to do an unofficial deal with the Communists. But the Bank of Portugal made it clear that Portugal could expect no IMF loan if Communist demands for recognition of their hold on agriculture in the Alentejo, and for measures to stimulate public sector employment and wages, were implemented.

The subtle strategy of Freitas do Amaral and Amaro da Costa, the leader of technically the most right-wing party, in keeping their lines open to the socialists, then began to pay off. The Centre Democrats hinted that they would be prepared to support a government which included some of their top men even if it was not officially called a coalition. Soares agreed, provided firstly that neither Freitas do Amaral nor Amaro da Costa was among his ministers and, secondly, that he could secure an unofficial deal with the Communists to support his government, to balance the picture. The Centre Democrats in return said they must not be linked to such a deal, and insisted on a stringent economic programme, granting credits to private industry and compensating those expropriated during the revolutionary period. When Soares passed the programme to Cunhal, the Communists flatly refused to support the government. Swallowing his doubts, Soares went ahead on 26 January and founded a new government containing three Centre Democrats—they were given the foreign ministry, the trade ministry and the administrative reform ministry to take the place of Freitas do Amaral's administrative commission.

With a much more coherent economic programme and finance minister—Vitor Constancio, the former deputy governor of the Bank of Portugal—the new government seemed to have a better chance of pulling Portugal out of its decline. Soares had at last decided to stop bridging the divisions within his party and had turned his back on its radical wing. How strong a challenge Lopes Cardoso or the Communists to the left could mount, first in frustrating the government's policies, and secondly in filching votes from the Socialists, remains to be seen. The Social Democrats' tactical ineptitude—at the last moment they had tried to join the talks between the Centre Democrats and the Socialists—seemed to be costing them votes to the smaller right-wing party. Opinion polls showed Freitas do Amaral to be second only to Soares in popularity in the country. The new government gave Portugal a good fighting chance in its tortuous road to establish a peaceful democracy. It will almost certainly be a last chance before President Eanes, under pressure from the right wing of his army, has to intervene openly.

Index